FOOTBALL'S
West Coast
Offense

FOOTBALL'S
West Coast
Offense

Frank Henderson

Mel Olson

Human Kinetics

Library of Congress Cataloging-in-Publication Data

Henderson, Frank, 1946-
    Football's West Coast offense / Frank Henderson, Mel Olson.
        p.   cm.
    ISBN 0-88011-662-5
    1. Football--Offense. 2. Passing (Football) 3. Football--Coaching.
I. Olson, Mel.   II. Title.
GV951.8.H445   1997
796.332'25--DC21

                                                        97-19424
                                                           CIP

ISBN: 0-88011-662-5

Developmental Editor: Kent Reel
Assistant Editors: Jennifer Stallard, Rebecca Crist
Editorial Assistant: Jennifer Hemphill
Copyeditor: Jim Burns
Proofreader: Sue Fetters
Graphic Designer and Layout Artist: Doug Burnett
Photo Editor: Boyd LaFoon
Cover Designer: Jack Davis
Cover and Interior Photographs: Courtesy of Brigham Young University/
    Mark Philbrick
Illustrator: Jennifer Delmotte
Printer: United Graphics

Human Kinetics books are available at special discounts for bulk purchase. Special editions or book excerpts can also be created to specification. For details, contact the Special Sales Manager at Human Kinetics.

Printed in the United States of America

10 9 8 7 6 5 4 3 2 1

Human Kinetics
Web site: http://www.humankinetics.com/

United States: Human Kinetics
P.O. Box 5076
Champaign, IL 61825-5076
1-800-747-4457
e-mail: humank@hkusa.com

Canada: Human Kinetics, Box 24040
Windsor, ON N8Y 4Y9
1-800-465-7301 (in Canada only)
e-mail: humank@hkcanada.com

Europe: Human Kinetics, P.O. Box IW14
Leeds LS16 6TR, United Kingdom
(44) 1132 781708
e-mail: humank@hkeurope.com

Australia: Human Kinetics
57A Price Avenue
Lower Mitcham, South Australia 5062
(08) 277 1555
e-mail: humank@hkaustralia.com

New Zealand: Human Kinetics
P.O. Box 105-231, Auckland 1
(09) 523 3462
e-mail: humank@hknewz.com

Contents

Foreword

Football, like other sports, has its fads. Each season the strategy used by the championship team becomes the hot new way to win. The Green Bay Packers win the 1997 Super Bowl. Now everyone wants to run this thing called the "West Coast Offense."

Actually, this offense is very similar to the one our Brigham Young program and the San Francisco 49ers have been running for a long time. That's not surprising since Packer coach Mike Holmgren has been an assistant coach for both BYU and the 49ers. What is surprising is that it took so long for everyone to recognize how successful this offensive attack can be when schemed and executed properly.

The West Coast Offense has many variations, but its core philosophy is that a team can keep possession and move the ball down field with a multidimensional passing game. Spread the field out, present the defense different looks, make more receivers available than can be covered, and get the ball to the open receiver. Sounds simple, but it's not quite so easy. That's where this book can help.

Football's West Coast Offense presents all the fundamentals for teaching, learning, and implementing this type of attack. Coaches Henderson and Olson have done a fine job of explaining and illustrating the key skills, plays, and strategies. It's solid information that you can use as the base or as part of your offense. Even if you prefer running over passing you'll find elements you can use to improve.

It sure helps to have a Joe Montana, Ty Detmer, Steve Young, or Brett Favre at quarterback, but the offense can be successful with less-talented players if they understand and execute. This book provides the base for that knowledge and performance. Read it, use it, and win big with it. But please, not against my team.

LaVell Edwards
Head Coach, Brigham Young University

Acknowledgments

The authors wish to thank Coach Mike Holmgren of the Green Bay Packers for reading this book and offering helpful suggestions and improvements. Green Bay has had great success using the West Coast offense. Thanks also to Bob McQueen for his support of this book and for his recommendation that it be "a part of every serious coach's library."

The authors are very grateful to the players and coaches who have contributed background material contained in this book. The many hours spent by the players practicing and implementing the thoughts and ideas of the coaches are much appreciated. Finally, a special thanks to Nina, Sue, and our families for their constant support and encouragement.

Introduction:
A Better Passing System

n the past, the knock against passing teams is that they had no consistency. You might win some games, but eventually a pass-first offense will come back to haunt you. Bad weather, a strong pass rush, lack of ball control, too many turnovers, and a host of other reasons were offered as obstacles to sustained success.

Through the '70s, this thinking was supported by the fact that the truly great teams ran the football much more often than they passed it. The Packers, Dolphins, and Steelers plowed through the NFL competition and Ohio State, Southern Cal, Texas, Michigan, Alabama, Penn State, and Oklahoma overpowered NCAA opponents. Game after game. On the ground.

However, the game was changing. A number of factors—foremost of which were TV ratings and attendance figures—led to rule changes that encouraged more passing, to the delight of pass-minded coaches like Sid Gillam and Don Coryell. Soon thereafter, Bill Walsh with the San Francisco 49ers and LaVell Edwards at Brigham Young University won championships with pass offenses.

What caught the attention of many observers was that Walsh and Edwards' offensive philosophy was unlike previous air attacks that threw only in long-yardage situations or to surprise the opposition. Instead, Walsh and Edwards' approach was to

- spread the defense over a much bigger area of the field, both horizontally and vertically;

- create mismatches in the speed, size, or number of receivers defenders try to cover;

- throw on any down and any distance to avoid tendencies that defenses could key on; and

- maintain possession through the air just as other teams tried to do on the ground.

These tenets formed the basis for what is now called the West Coast Offense. This high-production, low risk offensive attack has proven itself over the years and is now used successfully by many teams at all levels. Recently Mike Holmgren, who served as offensive coordinator for both the 49ers under Walsh and BYU under Edwards, turned what was a struggling Green Bay Packer franchise into a Super Bowl Champion using the offense.

The West Coast Offense appeals to high school coaches because it does not require players up front who can blow people off the ball, down after down, which is needed in a run-

A competent and poised quarterback is the key to making the West Coast Offense work. Here Steve Young prepares to take the snap.

based offense. And at the college level, where scholarship lim-
itations and strength and conditioning programs have helped
equalize the physical makeup of teams, the advantage of a
more wide-open attack is being demonstrated not only by
BYU, but Florida, Florida State, Colorado, Tennessee, and
other national title contenders.

The West Coast Offense is a finesse attack that features
both ball-control and big-play potential. Ball control in the
way of short, intermediate, and play-action passing results in
first downs, moving the chains downfield and maintaining
possession of the ball. Ball control works the clock and can
wear down and frustrate an opponent. A series of short passes
soon add up to sizable gains, putting the defense back on its
heels. Moreover, receivers who can run with the ball can turn
short passes into long gains or even scores. A big play can
change the momentum of a game and revitalize the confidence
of an offensive team.

The offense can employ any of five receivers in attacking
short, intermediate, or long. It incorporates a wide variety of
formations, pre-snap motions, and pass patterns. It utilizes

three-step, five-step, and seven-step quarterback drops along with sprint-out, rollout, bootleg, and dash actions. Because it is so multiple, the offense requires a thorough understanding of assignments, most of all by the quarterback. Someone on the level of Joe Montana, Steve Young, or Ty Detmer is hard to find, but a competent field general is essential.

This book shows you how to win using proven strategies and plays. The first chapter outlines the basic principles behind the West Coast Offense, while chapter 2 presents the strategies that make it work. The essential skills and routes of receivers and quarterbacks are discussed in chapters 3 and 4, respectively. The next chapter, "Pass Protection," focuses on the jobs of the offensive line and the backs in protecting the quarterback. Chapter 6 shows how to attack the defense, no matter what kind of coverage they present. Finally, chapter 7 is full of plays central to the West Coast Offense system. This playbook diagrams 20 plays against eight defensive coverages, and includes assignments for players at each key offensive position and tips for when the play should be used. It concludes with a section on play-action passes.

Teams that throw the football well are a nightmare for opposing coaches. At the same time, passing teams are fun to coach, play on, and watch. It's modern football. The West Coast Offense.

Although it's a finesse attack emphasizing ball control, the West Coast Offense also has explosive big-play potential.

Key to Diagrams

Offensive Players	Defensive Players
Wide receiver= $\bigotimes$, $\bigcirc$	Cornerback= C
Tight end= $\bigcirc$, $\bigcirc$	Safeties= WS, SS
Flanker= $\bigcirc$, $\bigcirc$	End= E
Center= $\square$	Tackle= T
Halfback= $\bigcirc$, $\bigcirc$	Nose tackle= N
Fullback= $\bigcirc$, $\bigcirc$	Inside linebackers= M, B, MC, MK
Tackles and guards= $\bigcirc$	Outside linebackers= W, S, B
Quarterback= $\bigcirc$	
Running back= $\bigcirc$	

Backpedal or less than full speed running

Optional path to run

Direction of movement

M

Block

Optional ball carrier or receiver

Continued path after block

Primary ball carrier or receiver

Motion before snap

Path of thrown ball

Quarterback dropback

The West Coast Offense Passing System

There are coaches who believe that if the ball is thrown frequently, the result will be a high turnover rate. However, we only need to look at the success teams such as the great San Francisco 49ers teams in the 80's and, more recently, the 1997 Super Bowl champion Green Bay Packers have had with this offense to see that it is here to stay. These teams achieved success because they followed certain principles to minimize risk while maximizing scoring potential. The following information makes up the foundation of the passing game system and must be understood when implementing this attack.

Principles of the West Coast Offense

There are five main principles to minimize risk and achieve success with the West Coast offense. These include protecting the quarterback, timing the pass, using multiple receivers (including using backs as receivers), reading the defensive coverage, and practicing the fundamentals.

Protecting the Quarterback

The offense must have a sound plan for protecting the quarterback. Pressure from the pass rush can result in loss of yardage and can disrupt timing between the quarterback and receivers, resulting in forced passes. Repeated hits on the quarterback take a toll physically and invite injury. The offense must have a plan to handle the rush of linemen, shooting linebackers (dogs), and defensive back blitzes. When the defense sends more rushers than available blockers, the *hot receiver* principle is used in order to get rid of the ball before the rusher can get to the quarterback.

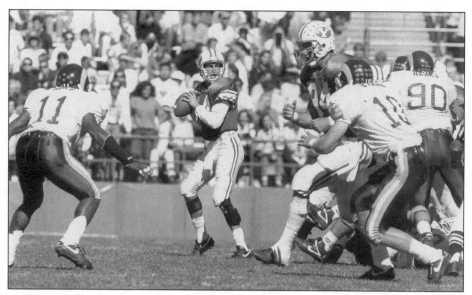

For the passing attack to be effective the quarterback must have time to set up and throw the ball. In this photo, Ty Detmer drops back into the pocket as he scans for receivers.

Solid pass protection gives the quarterback time to find the open receiver and throw him the ball. The quarterback gains confidence and gets into a rhythm of throwing on time while the defense becomes frustrated because of its inability to get to the passer.

Sound protection is based on effective blocking technique. Blocking for the pass is more than the offensive player positioning himself in front of the rusher. The rusher is surging toward the quarterback. The blocker must stop this surge and force the rusher to start up as many times as possible or redirect him away from the quarterback. Technique must be drilled in game-like situations and polished through repetition. Practice time allotted for pass protection should be proportionate to how much an offense will use the passing game.

Timing the Pass

Pass timing is the next most important element in successfully throwing the football. The depth of the receiver's route must time out with the depth of the quarterback's drop. If the receiver breaks into his route before the quarterback is ready to throw, the defender begins closing on the receiver and arrives at the same time as the ball. If the quarterback is ready to throw, but the receiver has not broken into his route, the coverage begins to converge to where the quarterback is looking and gets a jump on the ball.

Proper pass timing aids the receiver in getting open and permits the quarterback to get the pass off. It establishes a rhythm for the quarterback and receivers. A team that executes its passing attack with near flawless timing is difficult to defend, because in most instances, it simply beats the coverage.

The quarterback and receivers must have a thorough understanding of what a given pass route is trying to accomplish and how to run that route properly. Receivers must run routes at precise depths and adjust their route according to the coverage encountered. The quarterback must understand pass defense, recognizing the alignment of defensive secondary personnel and their drops into coverage. He must know the strengths and weaknesses of the coverage and which defender can take away a given route.

Using Multiple Receivers

The design of the attack must include a secondary or "dump-off" receiver along with a primary receiver. Their routes will complement each other so that (1) versus man coverage, a clearing action is provided by one receiver for the other, and (2) versus zone coverage, the defender must make a choice of which receiver to cover.

This design increases the chance for a completion, and permits the quarterback to get rid of the ball quickly, since he does not need to wait for his primary receiver to get open.

The receivers' routes should be in the same general area and at varying depths so that (1) a stretching action is made on the coverage, and (2) one receiver can come open before the other.

The quarterback can scan quickly from one receiver to the other. He is taught that when the coverage takes away the primary receiver, he will immediately go to the secondary receiver. Even if throwing to the second choice results in a missed first down, an incompletion or possible interception will be eliminated and some gain will be achieved. There's always the chance that the receiver might break away for the first down. Throwing the ball to the secondary receiver enough times will soon condition the defense to cover him, opening up possibilities downfield. The coach should give the quarterback a sense of when to throw the ball by having him drop back and set up, then telling him to get rid of the ball if he has not by the proper time. This will condition the quarterback to not hold onto the ball too long and get him into the rhythm of working from primary to secondary receiver.

The West Coast passing attack utilizes all five skill positions as pass receivers in a variety of ways when attacking the defense. By using all skill positions as receivers, the offense can attack the whole field and reduce defensive coverage into one-on-one situations.

A passing attack that does not use its backs consistently as receivers plays into the hands of the defense. When backs are kept in to block, the undercoverage defenders will drop and help on covering the tight end and wide receivers. Through film study a defense will learn the routes of the receivers and, upon reading pass, the undercoverage will drop to specific spots to cut off passing lanes. When backs release out on route, they control or clear out the undercoverage (see figure 1.1). If these defenders do not honor them, the backs become primary receivers, getting the ball quickly and then utilizing running skills.

Getting the backs out into coverage also takes advantage of the linebacker's aggressive nature. After a few dump-off or short passes are thrown into their area, linebackers will come up quickly to cover their receivers or make the tackle, opening up routes further downfield.

A final point to consider is that linebackers are run-oriented defenders who tend to play the run better than the pass. The heart of the West Coast attack is the completion of the short to intermediate pass in attacking the undercoverage, using all eligible receivers in the play to increase the chances for a completion.

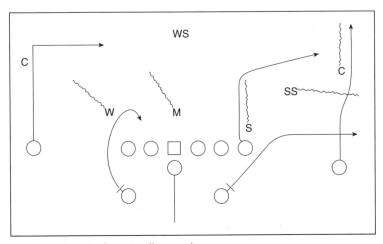

FIGURE 1.1 *Backs controlling undercoverage*

Reading the Coverage

The quarterback is taught to read the coverage so that an intelligent choice of receiver can be made. The reads must be kept simple so that the quarterback won't be hesitant in throwing the ball. Complicated reads look feasible diagrammed on the chalkboard but result in the quarterback being tentative and confused and holding onto the ball too long to be sure of his choice of receiver.

Reading coverage begins with an accurate presnap look. The quarterback scans the secondary alignment from one side to the other, noting the stance, position, and depth of defenders as they line up in the offensive formation. The alignment of the defenders will in most cases reveal the coverage.

After the presnap look there are two kinds of reads: (1) keying a defender to determine a strongside or weakside throw and (2) reading a passing lane.

In the former the quarterback reads the position or drop of a defender, such as the weak safety, to determine a strongside or weakside throw, as in the double speed out pattern. The quarterback presnap looks at the position of each safety in the four-deep secondary. He will throw opposite the best-located safety, which is the safety who lines up farthest from a wide receiver (see figure 1.2). The quarterback will work his progression of receivers outside-in to that side. If the weak safety were to line up to the weakside of the formation with the strong safety lining up tight to the tight end, the quarterback would work strongside (see figure 1.3).

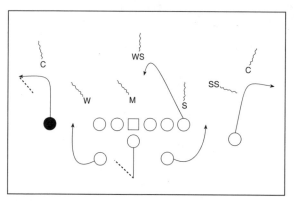

FIGURE 1.2 *Weak safety is the best-located safety*

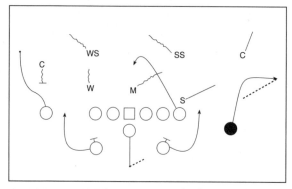

FIGURE 1.3 *WS lines up to weakside, SS tight strongside*

In the second kind of read, the quarterback reads the lane to a receiver, and if the lane is shut off, he immediately goes to his secondary or dump-off receiver (see figure 1.4). If one lane is closed, the other is open. The quarterback sees the relationship of defender to receiver and quickly makes a decision. He knows through practice and repetition which defender can take away the route, and so makes the right choice.

The concept of reading the passing lane is important because it eliminates the quarterback going to a secondary receiver just because a defender has dropped off into coverage. A defender dropping doesn't necessarily mean that the

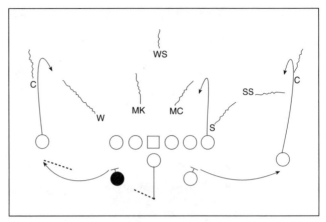

FIGURE 1.4 *Will linebacker drops to turn-in, QB dumps the ball off to HB*

receiver is covered. When the lane is shut off, the receiver *is* covered and the ball goes to the alternate target.

Designing the attack with primary and secondary receiver routes complementing each other brings four major benefits:

1. The quarterback gets his confidence up by completing passes.

2. The line develops confidence in the quarterback because they know that he will not hold onto the ball too long and get sacked.

3. All receivers will work hard to run their routes because any one of them could end up being the primary receiver.

4. The defense must work in covering receivers, knowing that the quarterback will not look for just one receiver and wait for him to get open.

The coach must design his attack with a progression of receivers building from the primary to secondary to a third or possible fourth receiver. The defense uses many coverages in today's football. It is unrealistic to think that a quarterback can identify every coverage and find the appropriate receiver. Having a progression of receivers as targets enables the quarterback to simply scan from one to another until an open receiver is found.

Practicing the Fundamentals

All receivers need to spend enough time catching the football. Receivers are made in drills that teach them to get their head around, watch the ball all the way into their hands, put it away, and run downfield. Running downfield must be emphasized so that receivers develop into ballcarriers once they make the catch. The quarterback must try to throw the ball so that the receiver can make the catch and run with it. If he can, all pass receptions have the possibility of breaking for big gains.

A commitment must be made to spend the proper amount of practice time in throwing and catching the football. Practice develops sure-handed receivers, pin-point passing, and great pass protection skills. In the West Coast offense, points of emphasis are

1. receivers catching the ball and running downfield,

2. quarterbacks throwing catchable balls,

3. the line developing pass-blocking skills to protect the passer, and

4. all facets working together as a unit for great pass timing.

Steve Sarkisian has set up, found his receiver, and is getting the pass off on time.

West Coast Offense Pass Formations

West Coast offense pass formations spread the defense out, creating possible one-on-one situations for the passing game and preventing the defense from loading up near the line of scrimmage to stop the run. These formations open up areas for all receivers to maneuver and get open for the pass. In the basic formations there are at least two pure receivers, the split end and flanker; a tight end; and two running backs, the fullback and halfback.

Player Formations

In the West Coast system the wide receivers are those who can get open, consistently make the catch, and run for yardage. Speed is a plus and running precise routes is a must.

At quarterback the coach looks for the performer, the one who can move the team. Setting up quickly and delivering the ball accurately with good velocity are skills essential to the position. The quarterback must also throw a catchable ball. Quarterbacks who throw the ball hard all the time make catching difficult. The ball must be thrown properly for the route being run by the receiver.

The tight end is a possession receiver and blocker. He must be able to make the tough catch over the middle of the defense and run to the ball on the sideline route. It is a plus if he has speed to go deep, since this forces two-deep secondaries to be concerned about covering three-deep running receivers with two safeties.

Beside being effective ball carriers, the running backs need to be proficient at catching the ball and protecting the passer. Throwing the ball to the running backs is good strategy, since they can receive the ball in the open, where there is room to use their running skills. Using motion can isolate a running back on a particular defender or move him to a position where he can release and go for the deep pass.

Versus an effective passing attack, defenses will shoot linebackers (dogs) or defensive backs (blitzes) in an effort to

In the passing offense, the coach can use any of five receivers in attacking short, intermediate, and long.

sack the quarterback and disrupt pass timing. Picking up a shooting linebacker coming up the middle differs from picking up one coming from the outside. Backs need to be able to identify these maneuvers and block them away from the quarterback. Successfully blocking this kind of defensive pressure gives the offense two major advantages. Many times defenders are left one-on-one with receivers, resulting in a big-play possibility for the offense, and the offense gains a psychological edge on the defense by handling their pressure tactic.

For the line, as at all positions, blocking is the key. In addition to run-blocking technique, linemen in this system must learn the pass-protection skills of setting up, body position, using the hands, and staying between the rusher and quarterback. Linemen must develop pride and a determination that no defender will get through to their quarterback. Defenders used to have an advantage in that they could use their hands, while the offensive linemen could not. The rules have changed, allowing pass protectors to use their hands in delivering a punch to neutralize the rusher and in diverting his rush. Therefore, the defense does not enjoy a decided edge.

Receivers

The two wide receivers usually split out, stretching the formation. The split that they take is determined by the position of the ball on the field (middle, left hash, etc.) and their play assignment. When the ball is on the hash, the wide receiver to the short side of the field will line up no closer than 5 yards to the sideline.

On passing plays receiver splits can be influenced by the strength of the quarterback's arm. For example, the ball must not hang in the air on the out route, so the receiver must not take a maximum split when executing this play.

When determining which kind of player plays which wide receiver position, some coaches will put their best receiver to the split end side. Most defensive secondaries will rotate or favor their coverage to the two-receiver side, and the split end can work against a cornerback and outside linebacker rather than a cornerback and safety. Other coaches want this athlete in the flanker position where he can be used in combination routes with the tight end and running back. He also can be used as a ballcarrier in running reverses and be put in motion for specific assignments.

The following are specifics for the wide receiver position:

Splits:

Tight...........................3 feet

Minimum ....6 to 8 yards

Normal.......................8 to 10 yards

Maximum...................over 10 yards

See figure 1.5 for wide receiver splits.

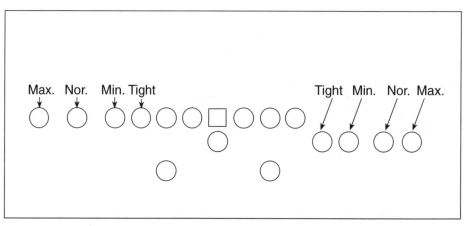

FIGURE 1.5 *Wide receiver splits*

Running Backs

In this text two back formations are emphasized because of their ability to protect the quarterback while permitting the wide receivers and tight end to release immediately on route. Many one-back schemes require the quarterback to read a quick or hot receiver, getting the ball off before the rush gets to him. Unfortunately, the quarterback usually takes a full hit even after releasing the ball.

The running backs will in general line up with their feet at 4 yards from the back tip of the ball. Some coaches who want to emphasize the run-to-daylight concept will have their backs at 5 yards, while others who want their backs to hit the hole and get out on routes quickly will go to the 4-yard depth. Quickness off the ball must be a factor when determining depth of alignment, and consistency of alignment is essential in establishing proper play timing.

As the backs line up they assume a two-point stance to survey the defense, noting the position of linebackers. Upon the quarterback's command of "Set!" they shift down into their three-point stance.

Linemen

Upon breaking the huddle, the center must quickly get set in his position so the rest of the players can line up off him. He will grasp the ball with one hand so that the other hand can be used quickly for blocking.

The guards will line up their shoulders on the center's hip. The tackles line up on the guards, and the tight end lines up on the tackle to his side. This off-the-line position enables the blockers to read defensive stunts. In short-yardage or goal-line situations, the coach may want the offensive line to crowd the ball to engage the defense quickly.

The guards and tackles line up with their outside foot back and outside arm down. This stance enables the blocker to execute pass

Guards, tackles, and the center are the first line of defense and provide the quarterback with a safe pocket from which to throw.

protection technique and help in the execution of combination blocks for the running game. There are coaches who want the guards and tackles to initially line up in a two-point stance, then upon the command of the quarterback, take their three-point stance. These coaches believe that by doing this, the linemen can get a presnap picture of the defense's alignment and possible intentions. Other coaches want the linemen in their three-point stance, ready to fire off the line.

Basic Line Splits:

Center and Guard . . . 2 feet

Guard and Tackle . . . 3 feet

Tight End . . . . 3 feet or according to assignment

On sure passing downs, the offense can have their tackles line up in a two-point stance to aid in their drop and pass-protection setup versus an outside rusher.

Tight End

With the tight end the offense has six interior blockers and a receiver that can be used in combination with either the receiver on the strongside (three-receiver side) or weakside (two-receiver side) of the formation. Upon reaching the line of scrimmage, the tight end takes his proper split and assumes his three-point stance immediately. When put in motion, he can be used as an extra blocker at the point of attack or as a receiver attacking a specific area or defender.

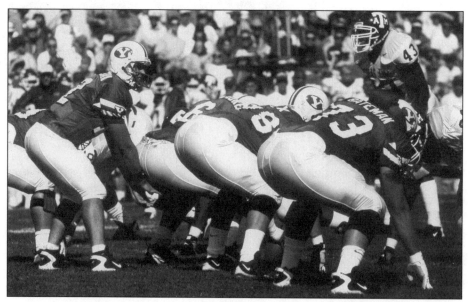

Presnap reads of the defense help the quarterback call the right play for attack.

Formations

In the following formations, the split end is X, the flanker is Z, and the tight end is Y. The halfback is H and the fullback is F. The term right or left designates the two-receiver side. The strongside or weakside of a formation is determined by the tight end. The side where the tight end lines up is the strongside while the side away from the tight end is the weakside. For simplicity, all formations will be called to the right.

■ Brown Right

In this formation the full-back lines up behind the quarterback. The halfback lines up splitting the inside leg of the tackle weakside. The call of right tells the tight end and flanker to line up to the right while

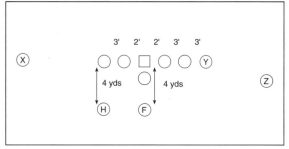

Brown right

the split end goes left. The strongside is to the right.

The fullback is a running threat to either side in the Brown formation. He can be used as a possible third receiver either to the weakside or strongside. The halfback can be used in route combinations with the split end, while the tight end can work in combination with the flanker.

■ Tan Right

Tan formation is a popular offset I alignment. The halfback lines up behind the quarterback, with the fullback assuming the alignment of splitting the inside leg of the weakside tackle. The halfback is 6 to 7 yards

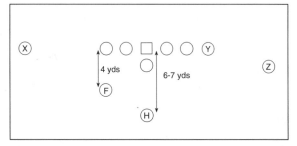

Tan right

deep, while the fullback aligns at 4 yards from the ball. The split end goes weakside while the tight end and flanker go strongside.

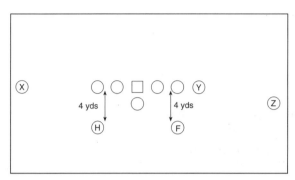

Red right

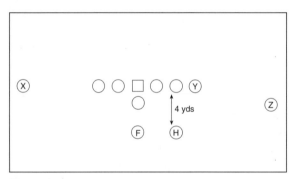

Blue right

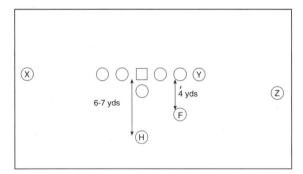

Purple right

■ Red Right

In Red Right the backs will split with one lining up weakside and one going strongside. Both will line up splitting the inside leg of the tackle to their side. Both align 4 yards deep. This formation is used when the offense wishes to attack the field with five receivers, and enables both backs to quickly out on route.

■ Blue Right

This formation is like the Brown except that the half-back lines up strongside, with the fullback behind the quarterback. It lends itself to power running plays strongside and to combination route pass plays with three receivers out strongside.

■ Purple Right

This formation is the offset I to the strongside. The halfback lines up behind the quarterback 6 to 7 yards deep with the fullback 4 yards deep and splitting the inside leg of the strongside tackle. The advantages of this formation are the same as in Blue except that the halfback and fullback have exchanged places.

■ Orange Right

This formation is a slot formation. Both wide receivers
go to the call side, with the
tight end going opposite
them. The strongide is still
the tight end side. The split
end lines up wide on the
line of scrimmage, while the
flanker lines up inside the
split end and off the line of

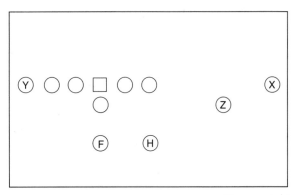

Orange right

scrimmage. In most cases the flanker will split the distance
between his tackle and the split end. The halfback lines up
weakside (in this case, the two-receiver side), splitting the
inside leg of his tackle, and the fullback lines up behind the
quarterback. When the tight end hears "Orange!" he knows
that he will be lining up opposite the directional call.

This formation allows the offense to work three- to four-
receiver combination routes to the weakside. Seven-man protection can be provided by keeping in the tight end and fullback. Overadjustment by the secondary to the two-receiver
side opens up running and passing possibilities strongside.

■ Yellow Right

In Yellow formation the split
end and flanker again line
up to the same side, except
the split end takes his place
on the line of scrimmage
inside the flanker positioned
off the line. The offense can
attack the same as in
Orange, with the split end
and flanker exchanging

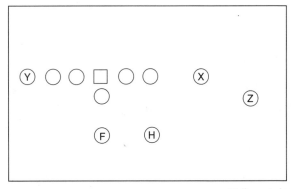

Yellow right

places. The offense can also run weakside plays with a strongside
look when the split end tightens down his split.

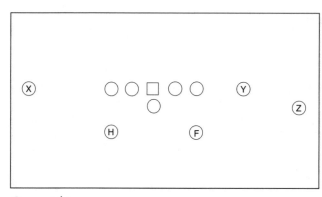

Green right

■ Green Right

This formation is one that is used chiefly versus an eight-man front. By splitting out the tight end, the offense can reduce the front to seven men, allowing better pickup of dogging lineback-ers. When "Green" is called, the skill players line up as in Red except the tight end splits out rather than lining up tight.

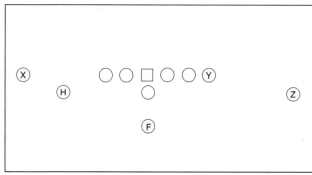

Black right

■ Black Right

When Black is called, the halfback breaks from his position and lines up in a slot posi-tion to the weakside. The tight end and flanker line up strong, the split end and half-back line up weak, and the fullback lines up behind the quarterback. The half-back can act as a third wide receiver. This formation can reduce an eight-man front to a seven. It provides strongside running while enabling four receivers to release immediately out on route.

The catch is everything. Toughness, in addition to speed, is essential for receivers.

Passing Series

The West Coast system varies in the number of receivers released, protection for the quarterback, and in the method of attacking defenses.

■ 40 Series

In the 40 series the tight end and both backs stay in to block for maximum protection when the offense expects a hard rush or when facing an eight-man front that repeatedly sends 7 to 8 rushers, leaving one-on-

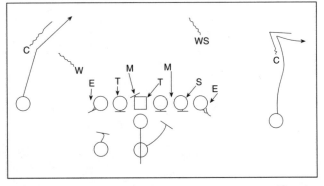

40 series

one coverage in the secondary. The wide receivers run individually-called routes.

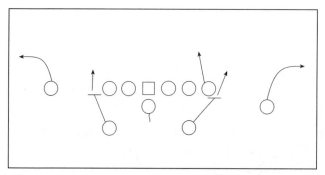

50 series

■ 50 Series

The 50 series consists of quick passes with the quarterback using a three-step drop. The tight end may or may not be released out on route, and the line will block aggressively to keep the defense's hands down. The 50 series permits the quarterback to gain confidence by starting off with a short completion.

Second effort and aggressiveness enable receivers to pull in hard-to-reach passes while eluding defenders.

■ 60 Series

This series has the possibility of all five receivers being out on route. The backs either check for dog before releasing or can be called hot and release immediately. The quarterback takes either a five- or seven-step drop

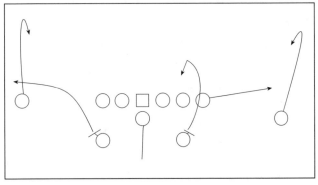

60 series

depending on the routes being run. The strength of this series is that it isolates defenders by attacking the whole field.

■ 70 Series

The 70 series is a weakside attack that can be run from Brown, Tan, Orange, Yellow, and Black formations. The tight end and fullback check for dog before releasing out on route. This series is effective in attacking linebackers, man coverage, and strongside zone rota-

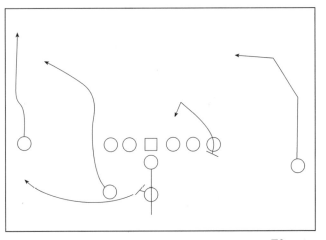

70 series

tion. Having the tight end stay in and block makes a very effective scheme versus eight-man front defenses.

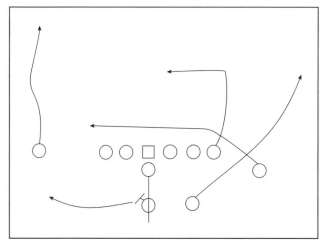

80 series

■ 80 Series

The 80 series attacks strongside with the strongside back releasing immediately out on route. The remaining back can stay in and block or release out after checking for dog.

Pass Strategies

In implementing an effective passing attack, the coach must understand how this kind of offense can attack a defense. Once this is understood, the coach can formulate his offensive plan, attacking the defense in a variety of ways. A varied attack is the most difficult to defend and utilizes offensive personnel to the fullest.

Stretching the Field

The offense uses formations to attack the defense by stretching the coverage alignment, isolating certain personnel, or rubbing a defender off a receiver. Formations with spread receivers give those receivers room to operate and to get open.

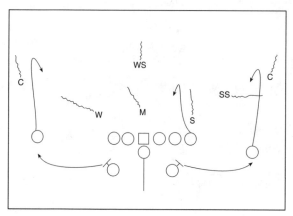

Horizontal stretch

■ Horizontal Stretch

Horizontal stretch means attacking the coverage widthwise. Receiver routes attack zones in their seams and dead spots. Versus man coverage, receivers control defenders, creating one-on-one situations. This attack is most effective against standard three-deep, four-short zone coverage or man coverage.

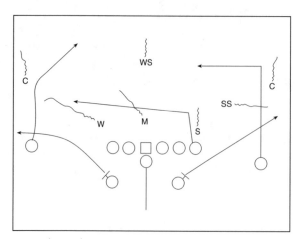

Vertical stretch

■ Vertical Stretch

These are all-purpose passes able to attack zone or man coverage. The strategy is that there are basically two layers of coverage (under-coverage and deep coverage), and the offense attacks these two layers on three levels: deep, interme-diate, and long. Versus man coverage, the receiver breaks and runs from the defender. Versus zone, the receiver will throttle down or sit out in the dead area.

With a myriad of pass routes at his disposal, the quarterback can keep the defense off balance. Here Jim McMahon eyes the defense as he calls the next play.

Employing Multiple Routes

By employing multiple routes, the offense can keep the defense off balance while attacking them from a variety of fronts. The following routes are central to establishing an effective pass program.

■ Delay Routes

Delay routes are very effective against zone and deep-dropping underneath coverage. Versus man coverage, other receivers clear out defenders for the delay receiver coming underneath, where he has the chance to run away from the defender.

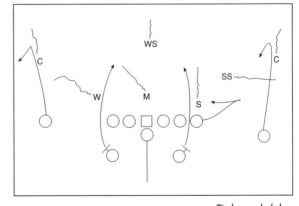

Tight end delay

In executing the delay, the receiver must be disciplined and exercise patience in coming off the line of scrimmage, allowing the undercoverage to drop and breaking underneath the coverage to the open area. If he is facing man coverage, he must break with quickness and speed to gain separation from the defender.

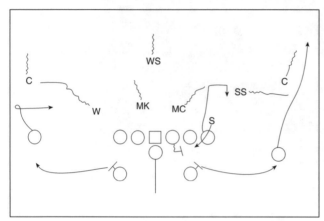

Tight end option route

■ Option Route

This route is a throwback to playground football. The emphasis is placed on the receiver getting open by reading the coverage on the run and adjusting his route so the quarterback can hit him with the pass. As the receiver releases out on route, he reads the drop of defenders around him. If defenders drop into zone coverage, he hooks up in the open area. If he reads man coverage, he breaks away to gain separation and runs from the coverage. When the receiver releases off the line and heads upfield, it is important for him to hug the nearest defender and break away from him, either hooking up in the dead spot or continuing to run away from man coverage.

The quarterback must read the area of coverage and anticipate what the receiver will do. He should throw the ball when the receiver establishes eye contact with him.

The option route is excellent versus a coverage like double man, since the receiver has great latitude in running away from the defender and getting open. Versus zone coverages, pass timing must be precise, since a quarterback who is looking at a specific receiver and waiting for him to get open can invite defenders to begin closing to that area. A late pass could result in an interception. With the option route there still needs to be a secondary receiver to go to if the primary one is covered.

The option route pass play is a great call in ball-control passing. It is a quick, short pass that can be used when the offense does not know quite what to expect in terms of coverage.

■ Shallow Cross Route

This route is a quick crossing route up to 3 to 4 yards in depth that allows the quarterback to unload the ball quickly versus dogging or blitzing defenses. The receiver sprints across and looks to the quarterback when he wants

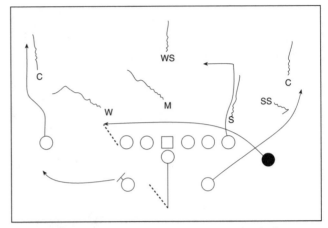

Shallow cross

the ball. Versus man coverage, he runs away from the defender. Versus zone, he runs all the way across the formation and sits out in the weakside flat. This route can be used in an effort to rub off a defender.

■ Snag Route

In the snag route the receiver releases inside at 5 to 6 yards depth as on a crossing route, then pivots back to the outside to trail and adjust to the coverage. This route is a short, safe pass allowing the receiver to sit out or run to an open spot in zone undercov-

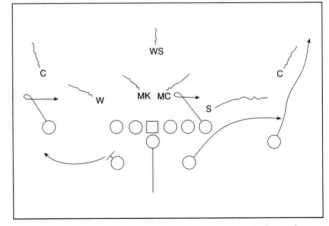

Tight end snag

erage and to pivot and run away from the defender in man coverage.

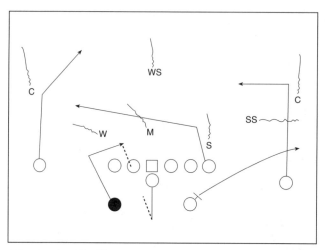

HB releasing "hot!"

■ Hot Route

The hot route allows the offense to release a back immediately out on route. On the snap the quarterback and running back key the defender that the back was responsible for picking up. If that defender shoots, the quarterback dumps the ball off to the back who is expecting the ball. This quick pass can result in a sizable gain because the back gets the ball so quickly. If the defender drops into coverage, the back runs his normal route. Using the hot route pressures the coverage immediately, increasing the chances of a receiver coming open right away.

Steve Young scrambles, looking for the open man. Receivers aren't the only ones who need good speed.

Using Motion

Motion is an offensive maneuver that can be very effective in attacking the defense. Defensive secondaries are taught to line up quickly so that they can key the offensive formation and look for clues indicating what play might be coming. They must be ready to execute at the snap of the ball, because gaining position on the offensive man is a big part of playing defense. Motion can be disruptive to defensive concentration. Secondary defenders may have to reset or to check or switch defensive assignments. While this is going on, the motion man can gain advantage in executing his assignment.

Motion can change the formation. Lining up the flanker in the slot position and then putting him in motion across the formation changes the formation from slot to a standard split end-flanker alignment. If the defensive back who lined up on the flanker goes with him, this could indicate man-for-man coverage. Whether man coverage or not, the defensive back must hurry across so that the flanker does not gain an advantage when releasing out on the pass.

The offense can be at an advantage when a four-deep secondary slides its safeties with the motion of the flanker who is going across the formation (see figure 2.1). In this adjustment

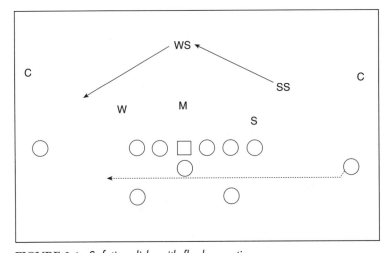

FIGURE 2.1 *Safeties slide with flanker motion*

the weak safety can end up forcing the run, and the strong safety, who is normally the run forcer, is responsible for deep pass coverage. With the sliding of the safeties, the cornerback who originally lined up on the flanker now lines up outside the tight end and assumes run force responsibility, creating a potential advantage for the offense.

Putting the halfback in motion (see figure 2.2) can stretch a zone or clear out a defender. This motion can indicate man or zone coverage. Motion can also be used to bring an additional blocker to the point of attack. Placing the tight end off the line of scrimmage and bringing him in motion toward the formation can accomplish this (see figure 2.3). For the defense double-team blocking is difficult to handle when both blockers come off hard close together. Defensive linemen are taught to read the offensive players in front of them, being aware of tight splits and linemen pointing in their stance. They are to broaden their vision to see the double team on reaction. In this technique the defender has a difficult time seeing the second blocker coming.

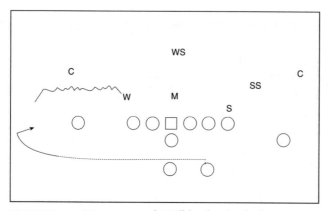

FIGURE 2.2 *HB motion with Will linebacker locking on in man coverage*

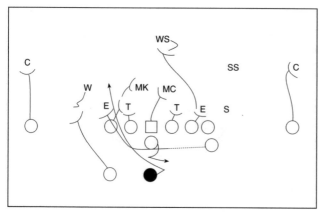

FIGURE 2.3 *Tight end motion on counter trap play*

When the offense wants to move a receiver to a specific point for release upfield on route, motion can be the answer. For example, the offense has a running back with great speed and good hands. The plan calls for lining up in Yellow formation with the flanker cutting down his split. The halfback goes in motion outside the flanker and, upon the snap of the ball, releases upfield on a takeoff route (see figure 2.4). The offense could have the halfback isolated on a weaker defender or have the area quickly cleared out for the flanker and split end coming underneath.

Motion can be used to force a change in who covers who in a particular defense. For example, when attacking double man

Receptions are the result of perfectly-run pass routes.

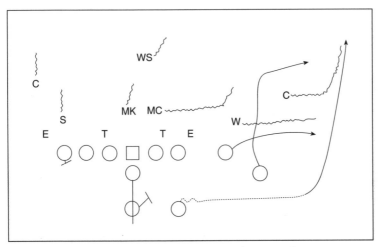

FIGURE 2.4 *HB motion stretching coverage horizontally*

coverage from a 3-4 defense, the halfback can be sent in
motion away and to the outside (see figure 2.5). As the back
goes in motion, the outside linebacker to that side, who would
normally be rushing, will check off to cover that halfback. The
inside linebacker to the weakside, who would normally be covering the back, must now rush over the guard. This is an easier
pickup for the guard.

Motion can also be used to move a receiver to a point
where he can release clean on route. A flanker put in motion
toward the formation and who releases upfield just before
approaching his tight end can avoid the defender and is in
position to get across the formation to the weakside as a
receiver. See figure 2.6

Finally motion can be used to free up a receiver from the
defender's bump-and-run technique versus double man coverage and to rub off a defender in man coverage, enabling the
receiver to release clean into the secondary. See figures 2.7
and 2.8.

Figure 2.9 shows different examples of motion.

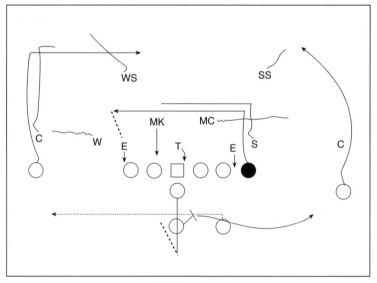

FIGURE 2.5 *HB motion vs. double man coverage resulting
in Mike backer rushing the passer*

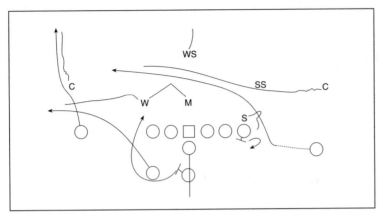

FIGURE 2.6 *Flanker motion to release over to weakside*

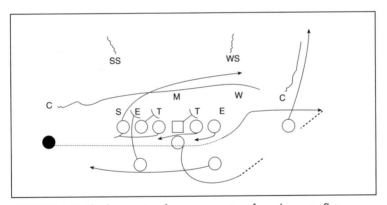

FIGURE 2.7 *Flanker motion frees up receiver for release to flat*

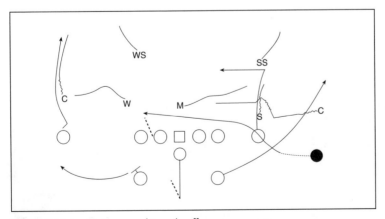

FIGURE 2.8 *Motion used to rub off man coverage*

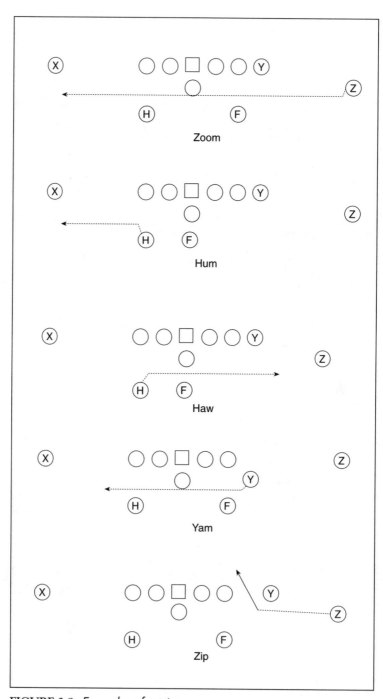

FIGURE 2.9 *Examples of motion*

Switching Receivers

Another maneuver that is available to the offense is switching the position of the split end and flanker. In the huddle the quarterback can say "Switch," then call the formation and play. When the split end and flanker hear this term, they will exchange positions with the split end lining up as the flanker and the flanker as the split end. This adjustment allows the offense to take advantage of coverage keyed to formation and aids the offense in isolating a receiver on a particular defender.

The offense can do this with the running backs by the quarterback saying "Change" then calling the formation and play. The fullback will line up as the halfback with the halfback assuming the fullback's alignment and role. This can add flexibility to the offense and aid in destroying player-formation keys.

Using a Hot Receiver

An essential feature of the West Coast passing attack is utilization of the hot receiver principle. When the defense sends more rushers than the offense has blockers, the extra rusher is controlled by a hot receiver.

An example is attacking the Split 4-4 defense which has four down linemen and four linebackers (see figure 2.10).

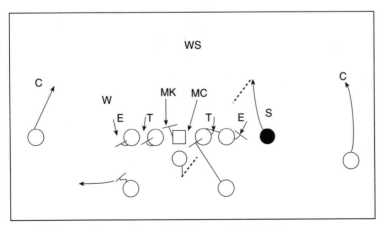

FIGURE 2.10 *Hot receiver principle vs. split 4-4 defense*

Protection for the line is lineman on lineman. The center is responsible for the weakside inside linebacker, the halfback for the weakside outside linebacker. The fullback has a dual responsibility. His assignment is first the inside backer and then the outside backer to the strongside. Since the fullback is responsible for two defenders, the offense has problems if both strongside backers shoot. So in all passes in which the offense is trying to get all five receivers out, the quarterback and tight end key Mac (the inside backer to the strongside). As the tight end comes off the line, he keys Mac and if he shoots, the tight end expects a quick pop pass from the quarterback. If Mac doesn't shoot, the tight end runs his normal route. The tight end must take a functional split so that he can release upfield and must work hard in getting off the line of scrimmage. When he sees Mac shooting, he must immediately look for the ball and make the catch. The quarterback also keys this same backer on his first couple of steps of the dropback. If Mac shoots, he dumps the ball off to the tight end. If Mac doesn't shoot, he continues the dropback and reads coverage.

After careful film study or if the coaching staff guesses dogging from an eight-man front such as the Split 4-4, the coach can tell the quarterback that the hot receiver is on for that defense.

The Tan formation can reduce the eight-man front to a seven-man front by having the strongside backer come out and line up on the tight end. If the strongside backer stays in to shoot (dog), the safety will line up on the tight end. In this situation the quarterback can key the outside backer. If he comes, the quarterback will dump the ball off to the tight end, who is the hot receiver. If the backer drops into coverage, the receiver executes the called route.

Receiver Skills and Pass Routes

For the receiver, catching the ball is the most important skill to develop. Possessing speed, running perfect routes, and developing great moves mean little if the receiver cannot consistently catch the ball.

A split end needs to release quickly to get a jump on the cornerback. This action forces the coverage to drop quickly, opening up opportunities for short passes.

In order to make the catch, he must see the ball coming to him. When the receiver breaks into his route, he must snap his head around toward the quarterback and pick up the flight of the ball. If he is running a crossing route versus zone coverage and sits out in the dead spot between defenders, he must turn his shoulders to the quarterback and pick up the flight of the ball being thrown to him. The sooner he sees it, the more time he has to adjust to the ball. He must not delay in doing this; balls are dropped when a receiver is slow in seeing the ball coming.

When he sees the ball, he focuses on the point of the ball coming toward him. He concentrates, using his vision to watch the ball all the way into his hands. The last two feet of the pass are the most important because this is when receivers tend to take their eyes off the ball in anticipation of running with it.

Once the catch is made, the receiver tucks the ball away and turns upfield to fight for yardage. Receivers need to learn to catch the ball with their hands whenever possible, not against their chest. With the fingers relaxed, the hands form a basket. As the ball enters the hands, the fingers give with it and close around it. The receiver must not jab at the ball.

Receivers must be aggressive in nature. When the ball is in the air, they must go after it rather than wait for it to come to them. Aggressive receivers make tough catches and make sure that defenders don't wrestle the ball from them. Interceptions can occur simply because the receiver does not fight for the ball.

Wide receivers must be aggressive in getting past bump-and-run defenders, accelerating up the field and in running their routes across the middle of the field. When running with the ball after the reception, they must learn to meet the tackler by dipping a shoulder and gaining leverage on the defender.

The tight end must be aggressive in catching the ball in a crowd. He also must have the courage to run his routes across the middle, getting past dropping linebackers bent on jamming him and disrupting his route. He must be aggressive in coming out of his stance and getting upfield. The longer the backer can jam him at the line of scrimmage, the less effective the tight end becomes as a receiver.

Obviously speed can be an asset. Receivers who possess speed have the potential to break a short pass into a long gain or score. But these players must also be taught how to run their routes effectively such as throttling down into the dead spots of a zone, in order to be complete receivers.

Teams that possess great speed at the wide receivers can force defenses into zone coverages. These defenses do not want to risk having to cover a receiver man-to-man all the way across the field especially if their pass rush is not strong. If these teams blitz frequently, the offense has the opportunity to burn them with quick passes that could break the distance.

After making the catch, the receiver becomes a running back.

Receiver Specialties

The keys to successful receiver play are (1) consistency in catching the ball, (2) precision in running routes, (3) quickness in breaking away from the defender, (4) ability to run with the ball after the catch, and (5) toughness in taking a hit.

Catching the Ball

Catching the football is perhaps the most basic skill a receiver must learn. There are six important points a receiver must perfect in order to catch the pass and advance the ball.

1. In making the catch, snap the head around and pick up the flight of the ball. Zero in on the point of the ball and watch it all the way into the hands. Remember, the sooner the receiver snaps his head around and picks up the flight of the ball, the longer he can see it and the surer the catch.

2. Catch the ball with the hands made into a basket. By extending his hands away from his body and forming a basket, the receiver can see the ball come into his hands. If the ball bounces in his hands, the receiver has a chance to regain control. If the ball comes into his body, the receiver can lose sight of it and if it ricochets, it usually bounces up high, resulting in an incompletion or interception.

3. When facing the quarterback and the throw is chest high or higher, the receiver catches the ball with thumbs together. For a low ball (waist down), the little fingers are together with the arms and elbows under the ball. When running to the left or right, have the little fingers together. The receiver should avoid bringing an arm across his body unless it is a last resort, since this can momentarily block his view of the ball.

4. When he is running downfield with the ball coming over his shoulder, the receiver will hold his thumbs out and little fingers together, reaching up at the last moment to make the catch. Putting his arms and hands up too soon will slow him down. In catching the long ball, the eyes are crucial. Few balls hit the receiver in stride. In most cases,

he must speed up or slow down to get the ball. The eyes must see so that the body can adjust. Underthrown balls are caught by slowing down, stopping, or coming back to the ball and catching it at its highest point.

5. After catching the ball, the receiver tucks it under one arm with the forefinger and middle finger over the point, keeping the elbow in to provide pressure on the rear of the ball. He squeezes it in toward his side and maintains this pressure throughout his natural rhythm of running.

6. Upon making the reception, the receiver's job is not over. Some receivers make the catch and then brace for the hit. *Great* receivers catch the ball and become running backs. Drill into receivers that they are to make the catch and then run for yardage. If they can break the first tackle, they will have a big play or even a possible score. In practice, drills must be run in which the receiver catches the ball and breaks downfield for 15 to 20 yards. With this mentality receivers will break short passes into long gains.

Receivers must catch the ball, put it away, and then run with it. They must be aggressive in executing these skills not only to make the catch and get yards, but also to gain the confidence of the quarterback. In crucial situations, quarterbacks want to throw to receivers whom they know will fight for the ball and come up with the catch. In crucial passing situations, the Dallas Cowboys' Troy Aikman will go to his clutch receiver Micheal Irvin for the big play, knowing that Irvin will fight to make the catch.

Running Precise Routes

Running pass routes precisely is essential in establishing the proper timing between the receivers and quarterback. Receivers must run their routes at the proper depth with a full effort so that split-second coordination between receiver and quarterback can be achieved. Split-second timing enables the quarterback to hit the receiver on his break from the defender or hit a receiver who throttles down into a dead spot in zone coverage.

Explosive speed and running precise routes enable receivers to get open and gain separation from their defenders.

Executing routes correctly enables the design of the play to have its desired effect on the coverage. Shallow receivers clear out undercoverage for intermediate ones; deep receivers clear out coverage for receivers running intermediate or short routes.

Breaking Away Quickly

All receivers must possess or develop quickness. Receivers who possess quickness present a big challenge to defenders who must react to their movement. They can use moves to turn the defender away from the direction of the break and then explode into their route, gaining separation from the defender. Versus man coverage, separation from the defender is the key for getting open for the pass; while versus zone coverage, quickness helps the receiver get to the dead spot or open seam between zones.

Using Speed

Receivers who possess speed offer advantages. Many times they simply outrun deep zone coverage. Defenses that cover man-to-man or even zone will play these receivers loosely, allowing short and intermediate passing. The defender's concern of getting beat deep will permit the receiver to make catches in front of the coverage.

Covering a fast receiver is a difficult assignment in man coverage. The defender is concerned about reacting to the receiver on his break and getting in stride with him. As a result the defender may overreact to the receiver's initial move. Seeing this, the receiver will counteract by using a move to turn the defender away from his final break.

It is especially difficult to cover a speedy receiver across the field. The receiver knows where he is going, while the defender must react and then drive hard to get in stride with him. Receivers who run shallow routes can release immediately across the field from their alignment, getting quick separation from their defender.

But speed can also be a detriment. Receivers who are fast may come to rely on their speed and not work hard in developing other aspects of their game, such as becoming effective ballcarriers after making the catch. Defensive backs are the last line of defense, and if the receiver can avoid or break the initial tackle, a long gain or score is possible. The quarterback can help by throwing the ball to the receiver so that he can make the catch and run upfield. If the quarterback makes the receiver stretch for the ball, the defensive back can give the receiver a damaging hit.

Taking Hits

Getting hit while catching the ball goes with the position. Courage and toughness are essential. Being aggressive while executing his skills enables the receiver to meet tackles rather than absorb them. He must not shy away from the difficult catch or passively go for the ball. The receiver must realize that if the quarterback has thrown him the ball, the quarterback has judged him to be open. If he were covered, the ball would have gone elsewhere. So he must be physical in making the catch. With each catch he makes against a defender, he is establishing dominance that can frustrate and lessen the defender's confidence.

To lessen the physical punishment on the receiver, physical conditioning, aggressiveness, reading the coverage and adjusting to it, and timing of the throw are essential. Physical conditioning is very important, since a tired athlete can't concentrate, cannot be aggressive in going for the ball, and invites injury.

Receiver Fundamentals

The wide receivers are premier pass catchers. Even though they will be called upon to block, emphasis is placed on getting open, making the catch, and running for yardage.

Splits

The wide receiver's split is determined by his assignment and the position of the ball on the field (middle, right hash, left hash). When a pass is called, the route the receiver is to run becomes a factor in determining his split. Generally speaking, inside routes are run from a wider alignment and outside routes from a lesser one. The quarterback's arm strength can be a factor. A large split causes the ball to be in the air longer, thus increasing the chances of an interception. If the receiver runs an out route, he cuts down his split, enabling the quarterback to fire the ball quickly to him. If the quarterback has a cannon for an arm, the split can be greater.

Taking a wider split on an inside route opens up seams in the coverage and allows room for the wide receiver to run away from man coverage. On a crossing route the receiver has a chance to read man or zone coverage and throttle down in open seams or lanes for the ball.

The receiver must vary his split so that a tendency cannot be detected by the defense. When a receiver is on the backside of a play, he can do this. Motion can also be used in disguising where the receiver will release into his route.

When the receiver is on the short side of the field, he must not line up closer than 5 yards from the sideline. If he is too close to the sideline, the defender can force him out-of-bounds, nullifying him as a pass receiver. Running plays can offer the receiver an opportunity to experiment with his split.

Stance

The wide receiver will take a two-point stance. This stance permits him to view the defensive secondary alignment and their stances in an effort to get coverage clues. From this stance the receiver can easily adjust his split. Versus bump-and-run coverage, he can change direction quickly when releasing off the line. If he is called to run a shallow route across the formation, he can see where the undercoverage defenders are and anticipate their drop.

When taking the stance, the feet are less than shoulder-width apart and staggered with either foot back. The knees are slightly flexed with the shoulders over the front foot. The arms are hanging down. After taking the presnap look, the receiver looks in at the ball, keying the snap.

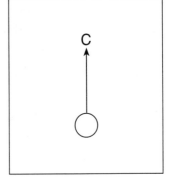

FIGURE 3.1 *Direct release*

Release

On the snap the receiver drives hard off the front foot, stepping with his back foot. He drives off low and hard, gaining speed in an effort to break down the cushion between receiver and cornerback. He must put fear of getting beat deep into the defender. This action forces the deep coverage to drop quickly, opening up opportunities for short and intermediate passes. Receivers who get downfield quickly are able to get behind undercoverage defenders such as linebackers, making it more difficult for them to provide coverage. As the receiver sprints downfield, he exercises proper running form with shoulders over the balls of the feet, good forward lean, arms pumping close to the body, and feet straight ahead.

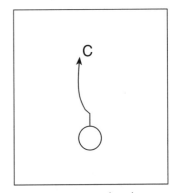

FIGURE 3.2 *Inside release*

The receiver will take one of three releases: direct, inside, or outside. In the direct release (see figure 3.1) the receiver drives at the defender's number or area of responsibility. If the defender lines up just inside the receiver, the receiver drives at the defender's inside number. On the inside release (see figure 3.2) the receiver comes off clearly to the inside and up the field to gain a particular advantage in the execution of his route. On the outside release (see figure 3.3) the receiver comes off the line of scrimmage clearly to the outside in an effort to gain a particular route advantage.

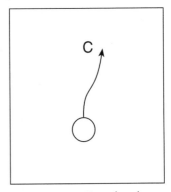

FIGURE 3.3 *Outside release*

When the receiver approaches the proper depth of his route, he can attempt to drive at the shoulder of the defender opposite his break. At this breaking point he can bend his knees to drop his center of gravity, keeping his weight over his feet. He does not want to lose speed. If he stops pumping his arms and raises up, the defender can anticipate his break. On the break he maintains his forward lean and puts on a burst of speed to gain separation from the defender. The receiver must run downfield hard and have something to give on the break.

Versus man coverage, the receiver can defeat the defender with misdirection or speed moves at the breaking point. On the break the receiver accelerates from the defender, gaining separation. He looks to the quarterback, expecting to be led on the pass so that he can make the catch and run for yardage.

As the receiver releases, he assumes that the coverage is man-to-man unless he reads zone. If he reads zone, he can adjust his route. Against this coverage he must find the throwing lane in the seam or hole of the zone and throttle down or sit out for the ball. At the signal for the ball (eye contact between the receiver and quarterback), the quarterback will throw into these lanes or holes.

On crossing routes receivers are not to look back at the quarterback until they have identified the coverage and are ready for the football. Eye contact between receiver and quarterback is again the signal to deliver the ball.

Releasing from the line of scrimmage is made more difficult when the receiver has a defender lined up directly in front of him. The defender may bump the receiver and drop into zone coverage or play bump-and-run man-to-man coverage. What's important is that the receiver must get off the line and upfield into his route. To do this he must surge past the defender, using technique to ward off the defender's hands. Bump-and-run defenders want to disrupt timing and harass receivers.

In releasing off the line of scrimmage, the receiver must not waste time trying to fake out the opponent, as this aids the defense. The receiver must not be forced wide, destroying his release upfield. As Tom Walsh, formerly of the Oakland Raiders, said, "The receiver must think of being in a phone booth with the only way out being directly behind the defender." In order to accomplish this, the receiver must first be aggressive in releasing with leverage and tight to the defender, warding off his hands as he bursts upfield. Once past the defender, he runs his route precisely.

The receiver can use one of two techniques, the *rip* or the *swim*, to ward off the defender's hands. The receiver must be drilled that when he makes these moves, he must also be accelerating upfield past the defender.

In the rip move the receiver drives off his front foot, stepping with the back foot. He drives off at a slight angle to enable him to get by the defender. At the same time he "rips" through the arm nearest the

Receivers must be tough enough to make the catch while being tackled.

defender, knocking the defender's hands off him. He performs the rip with leverage on the defender. He must be aggressive and make a strong move when releasing upfield to avoid being jammed.

In the swim move as the receiver comes off the line of scrimmage, he clubs with the off arm and reaches, or "swims," over with the near arm. He clubs, trying to swat the defender's hands off him. Simultaneously, he swims over with his near arm, bringing it down hard to eliminate the defender's hands as he accelerates upfield into his route.

Film study of the bump-and-run opponent can prescribe which releases would be most effective in getting past the defender. Whichever release he performs, the receiver must be cognizant of the fact that he must be quick in his move or moves and get upfield. One or two moves are all that can be allowed.

In defeating the bump-and-run defender (see figure 3.4), the receiver can (1) use a direct release to one side of the defender; (2) step quickly to where he wants to go, then away, then to where he will go up the field; (3) step one way to hold the defender, then release past him to the opposite side; or (4) move one way to get the defender to move the same way and then release past him to the opposite side. For example, if running an inside route versus a defender lining up in inside bump-and-run, the receiver moves outside with the defender reacting to him. The receiver then clubs and swims inside and past the defender.

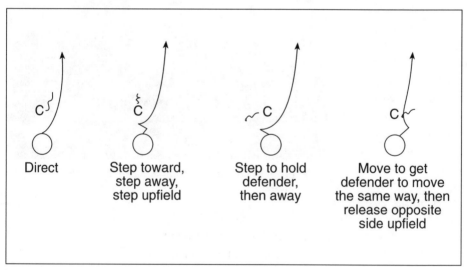

FIGURE 3.4 *Releases versus bump-and-run defender*

Wide Receiver Routes

A variety of routes are available to the wide receiver in the West Coast pass offense. They are shown in the wide receiver tree in figure 3.5.

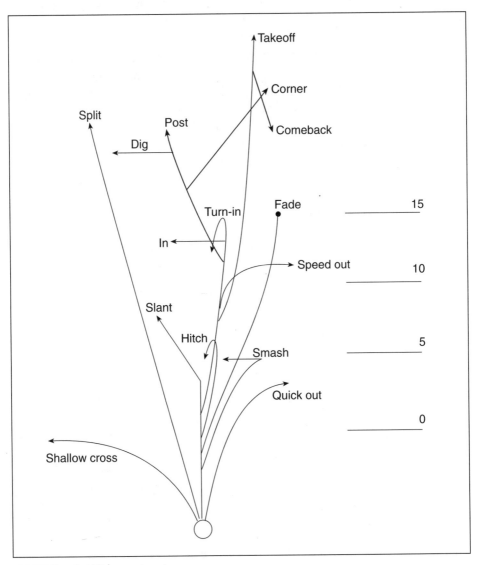

FIGURE 3.5 Wide receiver tree

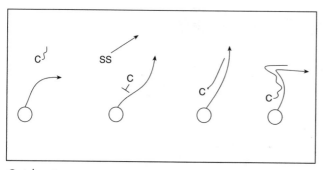

Quick out

■ **Quick Out**

In the quick out the wide receiver takes a minimum to normal split. On the snap he takes a direct release and drives at the cornerback's outside shoulder, forcing the defender to retreat quickly. At 5 yards depth he rolls off his outside foot, letting the route develop at 6 yards. As he rolls off that foot, he snaps his head around and picks up the flight of the ball. After making the catch, he works the sideline for maximum yardage.

Versus a roll-up cornerback, the wide receiver will turn upfield and run a fade route in the area between the cornerback and rotating safety coming to the outside third coverage. Versus bump-and-run coverage, the receiver will run the fade route aggressively. He can either use a direct release to the outside and upfield or fake inside and release upfield.

The quick out can still be run versus bump-and-run coverage if the quarterback is able to throw with the velocity to get the ball there on the break. When running this route versus this coverage, the receiver will bend his route inside, lean into the defender, and break to the outside.

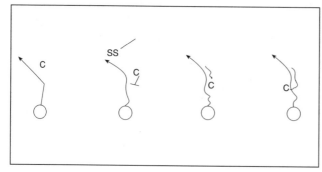

Slant

■ **Slant**

The slant is a quick route run with the receiver breaking sharply to the inside at 6 yards. The receiver takes a maximum split and a good presnap look, thinking about slanting into the seam of the defense. On the snap he takes a direct release full speed at the cornerback, forcing him to drop quickly. At 6 yards he plants his outside foot and breaks sharply on an angle to the inside, looking for the ball on the break.

Versus a roll-up cornerback, the wide receiver can break upfield without contact for the catch. Versus bump-and-run, he can take a direct release and make a quick inside break or fake one way and then release inside the defender. He must catch the ball running, break upfield, and put on a burst of speed to break away from the secondary.

■ Hitch

This route is a short one with the receiver breaking back to the ball at 6 yards. The receiver takes a maximum split and, on the snap of the ball, drives hard off the line of scrimmage in a direct

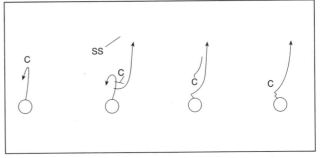

Hitch

release at the cornerback. At 6 yards he plants his outside foot, turns back toward the ball, and steps back to the quarterback. He must not drift. He will break either inside or outside away from pressure after the catch.

Versus a roll-up cornerback, the receiver will pivot out and turn upfield to the outside. Versus bump-and-run, he will fade.

■ Shallow Cross

In this route the receiver releases inside and crosses the formation at a depth of 3 to 4 yards, looking to the quarterback when he wants the ball. Versus man coverage, he will

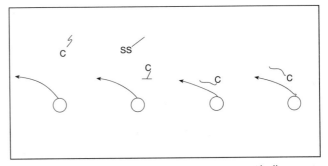

Shallow cross

break away from the defender, get separation immediately, and look for the pass. Versus zone coverage, he will cross the formation and sit out in an open seam.

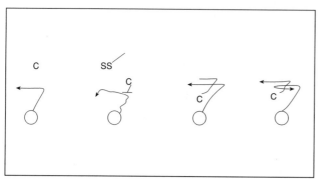

Smash

■ Smash

This is a delay route in which the receiver can break either inside or outside depending on the coverage. He takes a maximum split and on the snap of the ball comes off the line under control. He allows the inside receiver to clear an area. At 6 yards he breaks inside and reads the coverage. Versus zone, he comes inside and sits out in the open area. Versus man coverage, he stays on the move and comes underneath or pivots and works back to the outside. The quarterback will know to throw the ball when the receiver establishes eye contact with him. The receiver must not gain ground when coming inside. Versus bump-and-run coverage, the receiver pivots and comes inside, sprinting away from the defender.

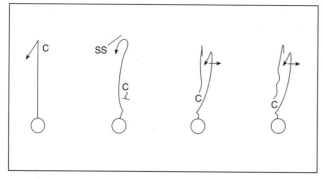

Turn-in

■ Turn-in

The receiver takes a maximum split to spread the coverage. On the snap he takes a direct release threatening the defender with the takeoff possibility. At 14 yards the receiver brakes by bending his knees. He plants his outside foot and steps to the inside over his original position. He snaps his head around and comes back toward the quarterback, gaining separation from the defender. He catches the ball inside the first man in the undercoverage. The emphasis is on coming back to the quarterback so that separation from the defender is achieved.

Versus a roll-up cornerback, the receiver releases inside, gets upfield while keeping his width, and breaks inside at the proper depth. Versus bump-and-run, he can use a direct release to the outside or a two-move release to get upfield to the outside. He gets the defender running upfield with him by selling the takeoff route. At the proper depth he plants his outside foot and breaks back toward the quarterback, expecting the ball to the outside. The turn-in route can also convert to an in route versus bump-and-run coverage.

■ Post

This route is broken on an angle slightly to the inside. The receiver takes a normal to maximum split. On the snap of the ball, he drives upfield in a direct release at the cornerback. He wants to drive the corner-

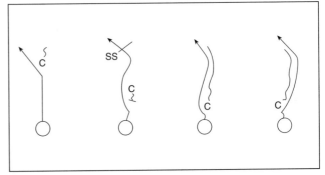

Post

back off with the threat of going deep. At 10 to 12 yards he breaks off the outside foot and angles inside and up the field.

Versus three-deep, he will hit the seam between defenders. Otherwise, he hits the open space in the middle. Versus man coverage, he makes a move and breaks past the defender looking for the ball. Versus a roll-up cornerback, he releases inside and gets upfield, running the route on a safety. Versus bump-and-run, he runs a tight, aggressive route on the defender.

■ Speed Out

Much of the success of this route depends on the quarterback's arm strength. The receiver takes a normal to minimum split. On the snap he takes a direct release at the defender, threatening the takeoff route. At 9

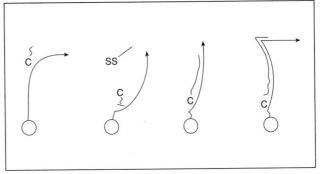

Speed out

yards he rolls off his outside foot and lets the route develop at 10 yards. As he breaks to the sideline, he snaps his head around to pick up the flight of the ball. The secret to this route is timing, so the receiver should expect the ball to be coming immediately after his break.

Versus a roll-up cornerback, the receiver will fade, getting to the hole between the cornerback and safety. Versus head-up or inside bump-and-run, the receiver can drive upfield or use a two-move release, bending the defender inside as if running the post, then breaking off his inside foot to the outside.

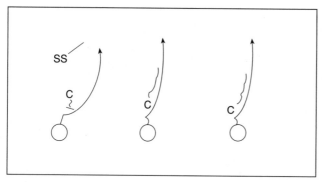

Fade

■ **Fade**

The fade route is one that gains the necessary width to clear cornerback rotation or bump-and-run technique. The receiver will take an outside release to try to avoid the bump. He sprints to the outside and looks for the ball over his inside shoulder. He must keep his width and fight for the ball.

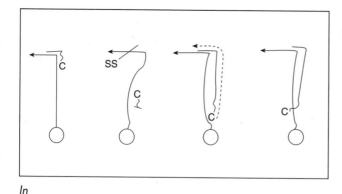

In

■ **In**

The receiver takes a maximum split. On the snap he takes a direct release at the cornerback and forces him to retreat. At 15 yards he plants his outside foot and breaks flat across the field, running away from man coverage and throttling down for the seams in zone coverage. This route can also be run at 12 yards or 18 to 20 yards.

Versus a roll-up cornerback, the receiver releases inside and upfield. He maintains proper width and at the designated depth, breaks across the field. Versus head-up bump-and-run, the receiver can use a direct release or a two-move release to get inside the defender and upfield. Against inside bump-and-run, the receiver can use a two-move release, starting upfield to the outside and then breaking quickly inside and up the field. As a second option he can use a direct release upfield to the outside and come over the top or allow the defender to overrun and come back underneath him.

■ Corner

The corner route is a companion to the post, with the final break going to the corner. It is a very effective route versus man coverage. It allows the quarterback space to complete the pass and, if run properly, can turn the defender completely away from the receiver's break.

Corner

The receiver takes a normal split. On the snap he takes a direct release, drives hard upfield for 10 yards, and breaks to the post. He sells the post move by quickly looking back toward the quarterback as if to receive the ball. At 14 yards he plants his inside foot and breaks to the corner, looking for the ball and being ready to run to it.

Versus man coverage, the receiver strives to turn the defender away from the break, then drives away from the defender to get separation. Versus three-deep zone, he adjusts his route to a circle when the defender stays back deep in his zone.

Versus a roll-up cornerback, the receiver releases inside and upfield and runs the corner route on the safety. Versus head-up or inside bump-and-run, he drives upfield, bends the defender inside on a post move, and breaks to the corner.

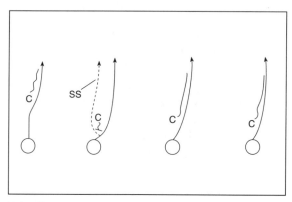

Takeoff

■ Takeoff

The takeoff is a speed route to get as much depth as possible to beat the defender deep. The receiver takes a normal split and, on the snap releases directly, sprinting at the cornerback to get on top of him. As he gets close, he breaks to the outside and past the defender. If the defender takes away the outside, the receiver can break inside past the defender but must keep his width. When the receiver gets to a depth of 10 to 15 yards and finds that the defender has maintained a cushion, he must either stutter-step or give an inside or outside move to get the defender to break down, and then burst past him.

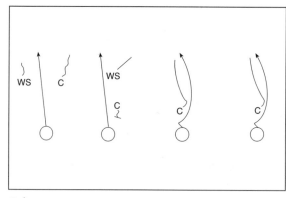

Split

■ Split

In the split route the receiver drives deep between the cornerback and safety to his side. The receiver takes a normal split and, on the snap, releases inside and sprints to a point midway between the cornerback and safety. Even though this route is intended to control defenders, the receiver could find the ball coming to him if the defender in the middle third of the field clears out and leaves the middle open.

Versus a roll-up cornerback, the receiver releases inside and splits the coverage. Versus bump-and-run, he takes an outside release and goes deep to occupy coverage.

■ Post Corner (Dig)

This can be a very effective crossing route off a post move. It can force the middle safety to drop in an effort to honor the post, giving the receiver room to come underneath across the field.

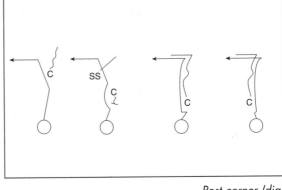
Post corner (dig)

The receiver takes a maximum split. He drives off the line of scrimmage and takes a direct release at the cornerback. At 10 yards he drives to the post threatening to go deep. At 15 yards (he can run the route at 18 to 20 yards), he breaks flat across the coverage. Versus man, he sprints away from the defender and expects the quarterback to lead him with the pass. Versus zone, he throttles down in the seams or windows and makes eye contact with the quarterback to signal him to deliver the ball.

Versus a roll-up cornerback, the receiver releases inside and upfield. Versus bump-and-run, he converts his post across route to an in route at the designated depth.

■ Comeback

This route is a companion route to the takeoff. The receiver takes a normal split. On the snap he takes a direct release and drives at the cornerback. He drives to the outside of the defender and upfield, getting the defender to run with him. At the depth of 18 to 20 yards he plants his inside foot and comes back to the sideline toward the line of scrimmage.

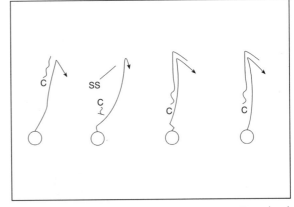
Comeback

Tight End Routes

The tight end is an integral part of the West Coast pass offense. Brigham Young University's Steve Young led the nation in passing in 1983, completing many of his passes to his tight end, Gordon Hudson. Thirteen years later Steve Sarkisian used two tight ends to control the ball while leading the nation in passing efficiency and directing BYU to the Western Athletic Conference championship and a Cotton Bowl win. The tight end route tree in figure 3.6 illustrates many of the patterns they used.

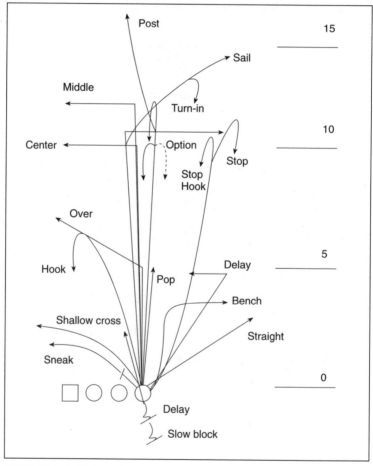

FIGURE 3.6 *Tight end route tree*

■ Pop

The pop route has the tight end releasing inside and catching the ball 4 to 6 yards deep. The receiver takes a regular split and, on the snap, explodes upfield. He takes a slight angle to the inside and is careful not to drift to the inside linebacker. He must look for the ball on release, as the quarterback will quickly put the ball right on him. The route is used in the hot receiver concept of handling dogging linebackers.

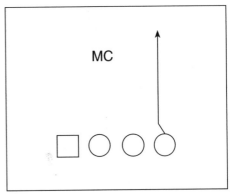

Pop

■ Straight

In this route the tight end releases to the outside, gaining no more than 4 yards depth. On the release he steps with his outside foot on an angle to the outside and looks for the ball. If he does not receive the ball quickly, he keeps running, setting down 2 yards from the sidelines at the proper depth. At that point he will turn and face the quarterback.

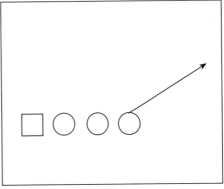

Straight

■ Bench

The bench route is the same as the straight, except the tight end releases upfield for 3 yards and then breaks to the sideline. He should gain no more than 6 yards depth.

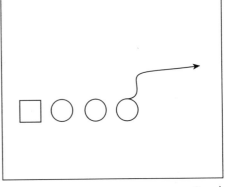

Bench

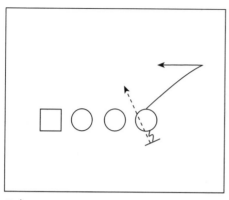

Delay

■ **Delay**

The delay route comes off a clearing-out action. The receiver lets coverage drop and breaks his route at a depth of 5 to 6 yards. He releases out and upfield and, at the proper depth, pivots back inside to the cleared area. He must not rush the route. After the break he comes under the linebacker coverage. He will catch the ball running, so it is important to not gain ground when coming across. Versus man coverage, he must make a strong outside move and quickly pivot back to the inside to get separation from the defender.

This route can also be run by having the tight end set up in pass protection, then release to an open area inside. On the snap he pass protects for three counts and then releases.

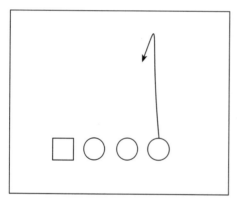

Turn-in

■ **Turn-in**

In the turn-in the tight end releases inside and upfield to a depth of 10 or 12 yards, depending on the depth of the wide receiver's route. He must not be driven off course. If an outside release is taken, he must not allow the backer to force him too wide and must get up the field to his designated depth. At 12 yards he plants his outside foot and turns inside, adjusting to the drop of the inside linebacker. The ball is thrown in aggressive fashion, and he must come back to it.

■ Over

The over route has the tight end releasing inside to 5 yards, then gaining ground gradually up to 15 yards as he crosses the formation. He must concentrate on getting past the inside linebackers and not being driven off course. If zone, and the weak flat is covered, he sits out in the open area weakside. If man coverage, he continues running across the formation.

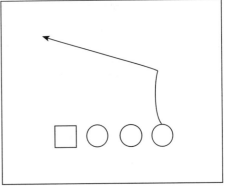

Over

■ Center

The center route has the receiver releasing upfield to a depth of 8 to 10 yards and breaking sharply across the formation. After releasing from the line of scrimmage, the tight end must drive upfield as near as possible over his original alignment. He must not gain ground coming across the formation. Versus man coverage, he continues running across the formation. Versus zone, he sits out in the open area to the weakside of the formation.

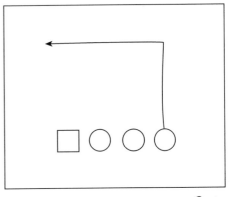

Center

■ Sail

This route is an adjustment route at 12 to 14 yards, breaking to an area versus zone and sharply to the outside versus man coverage. On the snap the tight end releases inside and up the field. He allows the coverage to develop. Versus man coverage, he fakes inside and breaks strong to the outside, running to the sideline away

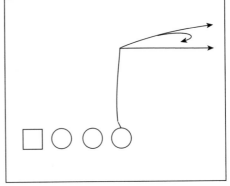

Sail

from the defender. Versus a cornerback up with strong safety dropping to deep outside third or half, run hook out in open area sitting out and facing the quarterback. Versus all other coverages, he breaks at 12 yards and takes this route to 15 to 18 yards.

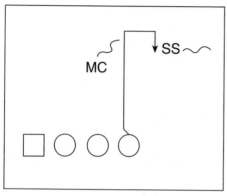

Option route

■ Option Route

The tight end releases inside and up the field. As he runs upfield, he reads the coverage and breaks away from pressure. It is important that he hugs the defender's coverage and then breaks to the open area. He does not want to release and run to the open area.

Versus zone, he will sit out in the dead spot, turn his shoulders to the quarterback, and make eye contact. Versus man coverage, he will make a move to turn the defender away from his break. On the break he gets separation from the defender and makes eye contact with the quarterback to signal him to deliver the ball.

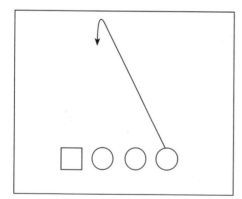

Hook

■ Hook

In this route the tight end takes an inside release, drives to his designated depth, and hooks up over the middle in the open area. He squares his shoulders to the quarterback and makes eye contact for the ball. This route can be run at 8 or 12 yards, depending on the play.

■ Sneak

This is a short inside route taken after the tight end blocks a defensive man. The tight end takes an inside release and blocks down on the defender to the inside. He may even go to the ground and then get up quickly. He will set up, run a shallow cross route, and look to the quarterback when he wants the ball.

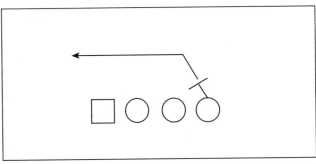

Sneak

■ Slow Block

This calls for the tight end to set up in pass protection to block. If his assignment drops off into coverage, the tight end releases out on route.

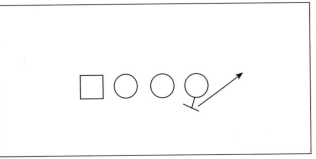

Slow block

■ Post

In this route the tight end releases inside and up the field. At a depth of 10 to 12 yards he plants his outside foot and breaks shallow to the post, splitting the seam. He must not lose speed on the break. Versus two-deep coverage, he favors the strong safety side and looks for the ball as he clears the linebackers.

While leading BYU to a national championship in 1984, Robbie Bosco utilized the post pattern to Adam Haysberg to defeat Pitt.

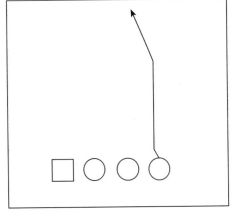

Post

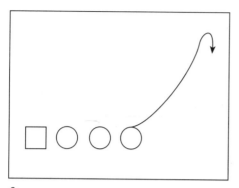

Stop

■ Stop

This route has the tight end releasing 3 or 4 yards outside and up the field. He reads the coverage as he comes downfield. At 12 yards he plants his inside foot and breaks into his route. Versus man coverage, he makes a quick inside move and hooks to the outside. Versus zone, he hooks out in open area.

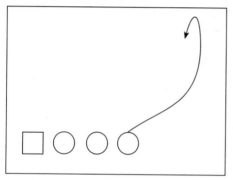

Stop hook

■ Stop Hook

This route is the same as stop except the tight end will hook inside. Versus man coverage, he can make a quick move to the outside and break inside on his hooking action, coming back to the quarterback. Versus zone, he'll find the open area and hook up, coming back toward the quarterback.

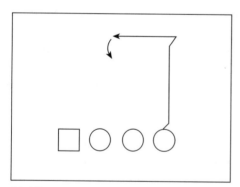

Middle

■ Middle

On this route, the tight end will take a normal to flexed split. On the snap he takes an inside release. He drives upfield for 12 yards and reads the coverage. He plants his outside foot and breaks across the formation, looking back to the quarterback when he wants the ball. He must break flat, not gaining ground.

Versus man coverage, he gives an outside fake and breaks across the formation. He gets separation from the defender and looks for the ball on the break. Versus zone, he breaks, looks for a hole, and sits out, coming back to the ball.

The Running Back as Receiver

In the West Coast pass offense, the back is featured as a pass receiver as well as a ballcarrier. When an offense has a back who possesses exceptional skills as a runner, it must utilize him as a receiver. The back who can avoid the first tackle or break this tackle becomes a dangerous receiver, and shifty or hard-running backs can turn short receptions into long gains and touchdowns. Robbie Bosco wrapped up BYU's national championship by throwing to his running back, Kelly Smith, to defeat Michigan.

When running backs go out on route, in most cases they are covered by linebackers. Against man coverage a back can give the backer a move to turn him away from the break, then accelerate on the break and run away from him. Versus zone the back may sit out or throttle down in seams to receive the pass. Once the ball is put away, the back can quickly turn upfield and split the defense.

In the multidimensional West Coast attack, running backs are often used as receivers.

The best way to open up the intermediate pass and control the action of the undercoverage is to throw to the running backs when the defense gives the opportunity to do so. Passes to backs are usually short, safe throws enabling the quarterback to get rid of the ball quickly. By varying the formation and using motion, a running back can isolate on a defender and use his speed and skills to get open and make the catch.

See the route tree in figure 3.7 for the variety of pass routes available to the running backs in this pro-style attack.

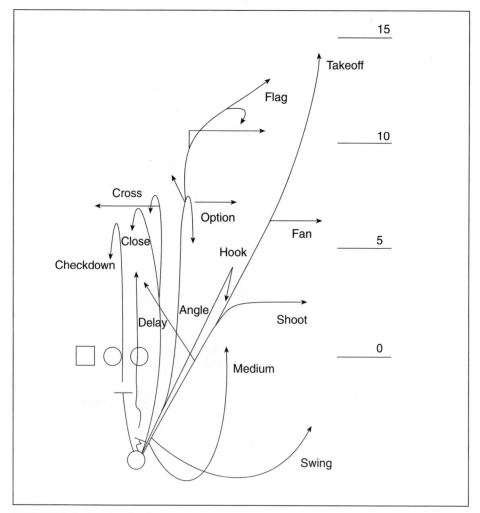

FIGURE 3.7 *Running back route tree*

Alignment

The backs will initially line up with their feet 4 yards from the back tip of the ball. This depth could vary according to both the quickness of the backs and their assignments. What's important is to get people in the best position to carry out their assignments in attacking the defense.

Stance

The back assumes the correct depth from the line of scrimmage and lines up properly in relationship to the other players. He is in a two-point stance with hands on knees. From this position he surveys the defense for an effective presnap look.

On the call of "Set!" the back shifts down into his three-point stance. His feet are even or with a toe-to-instep stagger. This position permits the back to move laterally as well as forward. If the quarterback wants the offense down in their three-point stances immediately, in the huddle he will give the command "Down!" Then he'll call the play.

Releasing out on Route

Unless the play calls for the back to release immediately out on route, on the snap he will set up to check for a shooting linebacker or defensive back. On the inside rush he takes a short step forward with his inside foot, then the other foot. During an outside rush, the back swings his outside foot around after stepping inside to stay between the quarterback and the rusher (see figure 3.8). If there is no dog or blitz, he releases out on route. He must be aggressive in getting out of the backfield and into the route, and he must be aware of any adjustments to be made versus man and zone coverages. The route must be run at the proper depth.

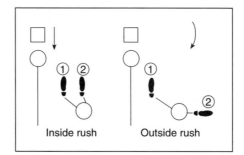

Inside rush   Outside rush

FIGURE 3.8 *Back checking for dog or blitz.*

Running Back Routes

There is a variety of pass routes available to the running backs. The following pages describe some of the routes employed by running backs.

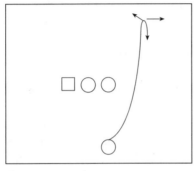

Option

■ Option

This route has the halfback releasing outside and upfield to a depth of 6 yards. He will read the coverage and hook up ver-sus zone and drive to the flat versus man coverage. He can break inside against an over-running defender.

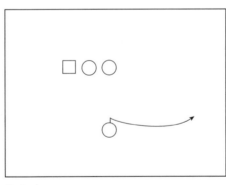

Swing

■ Swing

The swing route is a release through a wide arc. It stretches the coverage laterally and keeps it near the line of scrimmage. When the coverage drops off, the back can receive the ball and quickly square his shoulders to the line of scrimmage, enabling him to cut to his right or left.

On the snap the back will step up with his inside foot, then step with his outside foot. If there is no dog, he crosses over with his inside foot and begins his swing route. As he swings out he will lose approximately 1 yard. After 5 yards he looks back for the ball over his inside shoulder. He swings out to the flat, and as he approaches the line of scrimmage, he will stop and face the quarterback.

■ Close Hook

In this route the back releases upfield, hooking up in the open area past the line of scrimmage at 5 yards. He must take a presnap look to determine his best release and be ready to fight through traffic in order to get out. As he releases through the line and gets to his depth, he turns to the inside and hooks up.

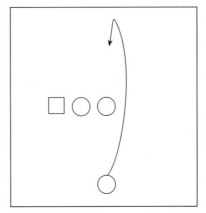

Close hook

■ Medium

This route has the back releasing toward a point dividing the distance between Y and Z or X and the tackle to that side. He gives ground on the release and when he reaches his breaking point heads upfield, looking for the ball over his inside shoulder.

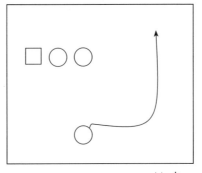

Medium

■ Hook

In the hook the back releases out at a 45-degree angle and hooks up away from the undercoverage defender. He hooks up 3 to 6 yards deep, although he could hook up as deep as 8 yards, depending on the wide receiver's route.

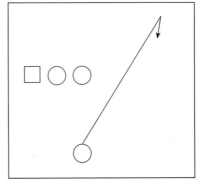

Hook

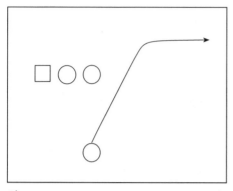

Shoot

■ **Shoot**

In executing the shoot route, the back releases at the outside shoulder of the linebacker to a point 3 yards downfield. At that depth he breaks parallel to the line of scrimmage at full speed and looks for the ball over his outside shoulder. As the back approaches the sideline, he will stop and face the quarterback.

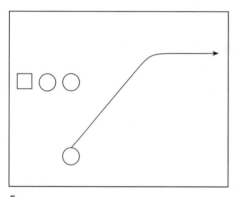

Fan

■ **Fan**

The fan is like the shoot route except that it is run deeper. At 6 yards the back breaks at a 90-degree angle to the sideline and looks for the ball over his outside shoulder. As he approaches the sideline he will stop and face the quarterback. The shoot and fan routes force the undercoverage to cover the back immediately or face a back receiving the ball while running in the open field.

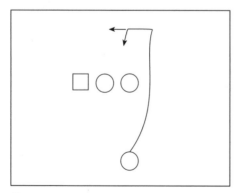

Cross

■ **Cross**

In this route the back releases out on a close route and continues upfield for 5 to 6 yards. Upon reaching that depth, versus man coverage he will drive across and parallel to the line of scrimmages or against the zone will pull up and sit out in the dead spot.

■ Delay

This route is run versus deep-dropping undercoverage. The back sets up for pass protection for three counts, then releases through the line and looks for the ball immediately after clearing the line of scrimmage.

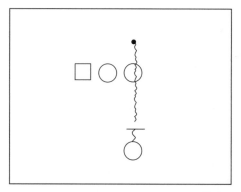

Delay

■ Check-down

This route has the back check for a dogging linebacker and then release between the guard and tackle, hooking up 5 to 6 yards downfield.

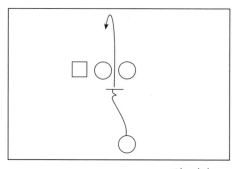

Checkdown

■ Angle

In the angle route the back breaks to the outside as if he were running a shoot route. At 2 to 3 yards depth he plants his outside foot and breaks on an angle to the inside. Versus man coverage he breaks away from his defender. Versus zone he hits the seam between defenders.

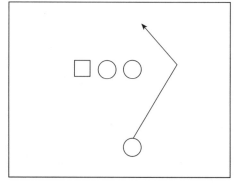

Angle

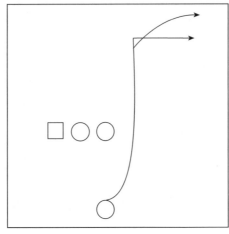

Flag

■ Flag

On this route the back releases upfield on a close route for 10 yards and then breaks on a 45-degree angle to the sideline. He looks for the ball over his outside shoulder. Versus any zone coverage, he runs his flag route. Versus man coverage, he converts his route to an out.

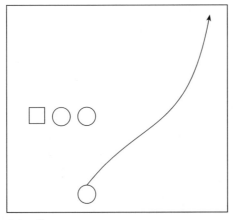

Takeoff

■ Takeoff

The running back releases from the backfield and sprints deep to the sidelines, getting no closer to the sideline than 5 yards.

Quarterback Skills and Throwing Targets

For a quarterback to be successful, he must possess leadership qualities and be well-schooled in the fundamentals of the position. He must know and understand the offense thoroughly since, in many cases, he will be a coach on the field. Even though the position carries great responsibility, he must not be made to feel that the success of the offense rests solely on his shoulders. This would only add to the pressure of playing the position. The quarterback should strive for consistency in leadership, huddle discipline, and skill performance.

The quarterback leads best by example. He should be a hard worker and a competitor. He must possess an inner belief that he can lead the team and relay this to them. He should enjoy taking charge, and speak with authority and conviction in the huddle. The quarterback should view each practice session as an opportunity to gain the confidence of the team through the poise he exhibits and the way he practices. This will solidify his position as leader.

Poise, leadership, and all-around athletic talent are essential for the quarterback.

Checklist for Rating a Quarterback

1. Accuracy
2. Velocity of throw
3. Consistency in throwing the ball effectively
4. Arm strength
5. Passing long
6. Passing medium
7. Passing short
8. Quickness in setting up
9. Release of ball
10. Poise in pocket
11. Scrambling ability
12. Toughness
13. Ability to move the team
14. Understanding the offense

Quarterback Fundamentals

In evaluating quarterback candidates, the coach looks for the performer, the one who can move the chains and get the score. The coach must not make his selection by who throws the longest or hardest ball, or the prettiest spiral. Quarterbacks who throw every pass with the same zip make catching difficult. They must learn to throw a catchable ball. The velocity of the throw will vary according to the route being run.

In evaluating quarterbacks, the coach notes who is consistent in setting up, reading the coverage, finding the open receiver, and throwing a catchable ball. A quick release is an advantage, since this kind of delivery gives defenders less time to react to a throw.

If the coach finds himself without a legitimate candidate at the position, he should select the best athlete from among his skill-position players and develop him into a quarterback. Usually this candidate has the respect of his teammates because of his ability, and he possesses the coordination, confidence, and competitiveness to learn the position.

Stance

The quarterback takes his stance with his feet shoulder-width apart and parallel, and slightly pigeon-toed to aid in pushing off on the first step. His weight is on the balls of his feet. His knees are flexed, adjusting to the height of the center. When the quarterback is working without a center, he can take a 45-degree flex in his knees when assuming his stance. His back is straight, shoulders parallel to the line of scrimmage and in front of the hips. His head is up surveying the defense. When viewing the defense (presnap look), the quarterback must scan from left to right and back, making this his routine down after down. He does not want to look at the point of attack and give the defense a key.

The quarterback's hands are placed beneath the center with the heels of the hands together and the fingers spread to form a V. His thumbs are together. The passing hand is the upper hand. It is placed with the palm parallel to the ground, wrist deep, with the middle finger in line with the cleavage of the center's rear end. This hand has a very slight upward cock in the wrist to give the center target pressure. The bottom hand secures the snap. It is held at a 90-degree angle to the upper hand. With the fingers spread, the bottom hand wraps around the ball. Anytime the quarterback puts his hands under the center, they must be open with the fingers spread so that he does not jam or break a finger if the center mistakenly snaps the ball early.

At the snap the quarterback secures the ball with both hands. This is his first responsibility. The fingers of his top hand cover the laces, while his bottom hand secures the ball. The quarterback must have the ball solidly in his hands before attempting to drop back.

Dropback

After securing the snap, a right-handed passer pushes off his left foot while stepping with his right foot. This is for a right-handed passer. This first step is taken for depth and is brought in line behind the left foot so that the drop is straight back. The coach should not allow any false stepping that could affect pass timing when beginning the dropback.

As the first step is taken, the quarterback turns. The right foot, hips, shoulders, and elbow come around on the lead side to get speed and momentum away from the line of scrimmage. With the first step the ball is brought to the right armpit so that the quarterback can move into his drop. The ball is held with both hands at jersey number height. The elbows are down, creating a relaxed, natural, pendulum action with the arms to generate momentum. As the quarterback drops, he looks over his left shoulder to read the defense.

In dropping back, the quarterback must (1) secure the ball and seat it properly by carrying it with both hands, (2) drop back to his launch point quickly enough to permit him the maximum time to pass, and (3) drop with depth to insure proper pass timing. Quickness and depth in the dropback enable the quarterback to get the pass off before a shooting linebacker or defensive back can pursue him.

For quick passes the quarterback uses a three-step drop. He opens, crosses over, and sets. When a right-handed passer is throwing to the left, he can take his last step slightly to the right. When throwing to the right, he should take the last step slightly to the left. This enables the quarterback to square his hips to the target and get the throw off quickly. These kinds of throws are strictly timing routes. Because the quarterback is not taking a deep drop, it is imperative that his rhythm be 1-2-3-throw.

Quickness and depth in the dropback enable the quarterback to pass before a shooting linebacker can pursue him. Here Ty Detmer prepares to pass.

The five-step drop is used for timing routes that get 10 to 12 yards in depth. The five-step drop can be taken with a hitch step forward such as when throwing the takeoff route. In this drop the quarterback is attempting to get 7 yards' depth out of five steps. In executing this drop, the quarterback opens, crosses over, opens, balance steps, and sets. The last two steps are slightly shorter so the quarterback can balance up and brake.

In the seven-step drop the quarterback is striving to get 9 yards' depth. This drop is used for routes that take time to develop. In performing this drop, the quarterback opens, crosses over, opens, crosses over, opens, balance steps, and sets. Balancing up and setting keep the quarterback from overextending on his last step, then having to gather up to step forward into his throw. Once the drop is completed, the quarterback can hitch-step up into his throw so that he transfers his weight from his back foot to his front foot.

The quarterback must work endlessly on his dropback mechanics, because as he begins to learn the offense he becomes focused into reading coverages, and his dropback fundamentals may begin to suffer. The coach must be especially concerned that he carries the ball properly and get the necessary depth out of his drop.

Throwing the Football

The throw begins with the grip. Many people place the little finger near the middle of the ball with the first joint on the laces. The index finger is near the tip of the ball. The middle finger is either against or across the laces, while the third finger extends across the laces. Hand size is a factor here, but what is important is that the grip is comfortable and not forced. The ball is gripped comfortably with fingertip pressure on the surface and a space between the ball and the palm of the hand. The nonpassing hand rests on the underside of the ball.

The quarterback completes his drop by stopping on the inside of his back foot. He is perpendicular to the line of scrimmage. His feet are directly under his hips. In beginning the throw, the quarterback pushes off his back foot and steps toward his target with his front foot. He must not overstride, as he wants to stay on top of the left foot throughout the passing motion. The step of the left foot initiates the weight transfer essential in getting the hips into the throw.

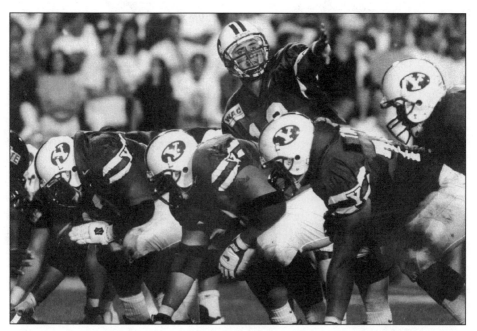

Because the West Coast Offense is so multiple, the quarterback must have a thorough understanding of assignments.

As the step forward is taken, the front hand pushes the ball back and then releases from it. The throwing arm cocks back behind the helmet. It is held high so that the elbow does not drop below shoulder level. As the throw begins, the non-passing arm is pulled down and back as the hips, followed by the trunk and shoulders, come around square. The elbow leads the way as the forward arm motion begins. The forearm comes over the top of the elbow and extends toward the target. The index finger leaves the ball with the palm facing the target. The thumb and wrist are snapped down as the follow-through brings the arm naturally across the body.

The quarterback will throw with some flexion in his front leg. Throwing with the leg locked out diminishes the weight transfer from back to forward into the throw. In throwing to the left and right, the quarterback must be sure to step so that his hips are square to the receiver. This allows him to throw with accuracy and velocity.

Through repetition the quarterback develops a consistent and smooth dropback and throwing motion. He is able to throw so that the receiver can make the catch and run for yardage. The photos in the Technique Forum on pages 80 and 81 illustrate the fundamentals of the quarterback stance, dropback, and throw.

Passer's Checklist

1. Flex knees in stance

2. Secure snap

3. Seat ball

4. Sprint back and locate key or keys

5. Set up at proper depth

6. Balance up

7. Step toward target and deliver ball

8. Throw ball to receiver so that he can run with it

9. Never throw late or force the ball into the coverage

Technique Forum

Quarterback Stance, Dropback, and Throw

1. The quarterback lines up to take the snap from the center with knees bent and a slightly staggered stance. He maintains firm pressure on the butt of the center, while keeping his head up as he calls the cadence loud and clear.

2. The QB receives the snap, secures the football, and begins his drop.

3. Backpedaling to get his depth, the QB brings the ball to a throwing position.

4. *After striding back quickly to set up, the QB scans for receivers before stepping up in the pocket to throw.*

5. *With eyes on the target as he has progressed through his reads, the QB puts his weight on his back foot, ready to step up to pass.*

6. *When releasing the football, the QB keeps his body square to the line of scrimmage and keeps the body balanced.*

7. *After releasing the football, the QB keeps the wrist in a pronated position and completes the follow-through with the arm crossing the body.*

Throwing Targets

The following ten pass routes are staples of the West Coast offense. Quarterbacks should know these routes inside and out, and should be aware that each may require a different setup, ball delivery, and timing.

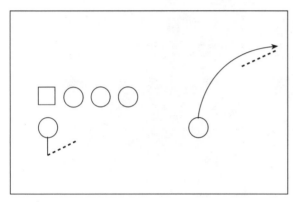

Quick out

■ Quick Out

The quarterback will zip the ball to the outside of the receiver, throwing on a line through the receiver's hip, keeping the ball low and away from the defender. A quick setup is necessary to the success of the throw. If the ball hangs or is late getting to the receiver, it will be intercepted.

Quarterback Gary Sheide led BYU to a WAC championship by utilizing the short passing game. In one game his wide receiver, Jay Miller, caught 22 passes, many of them quick outs.

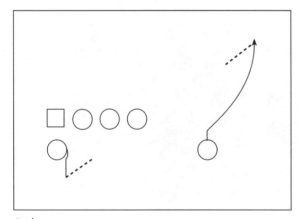

Fade

■ Fade

The quarterback will throw the ball over the receiver's inside shoulder. Throwing the ball over the outside shoulder causes it to go too far to the outside, but hanging the ball *too* far to the inside can be a problem if a safety can get over to intercept it.

■ Slant

The quarterback must set up quickly and put the ball on the receiver as he slants inside. He must not lead the receiver to where he stretches him out and exposes him to a hit by the defense. For this route to be effective it must be run aggressively, and if the quarterback makes a habit of stretching the receiver out, that receiver will not run it aggressively. The quarterback must not throw behind the receiver, as this will result in an incompletion or interception.

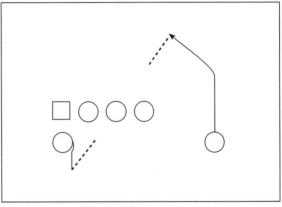

Slant

■ Turn-in

The ball must be zipped to the receiver at number level or lower. Too low a throw will not allow the receiver to run with the ball. A high throw can result in a tipped ball or a hit on the receiver who stretches out for it. When the turn-in is overthrown, the result will be an interception or the receiver being left in a vulnerable position reaching for the ball.

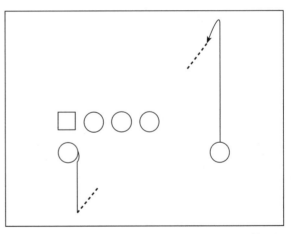

Turn-in

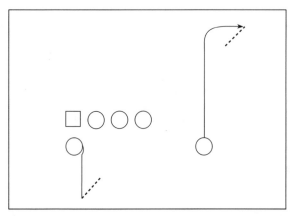

Speed out

■ Speed Out

Proper timing is crucial to the success of this route, so the quarterback must set up quickly. The ball must be zipped to the outside on a line through the receiver's hip. A ball that hangs or is thrown late will be intercepted. The quarterback's arm strength must figure into how wide the receiver splits out.

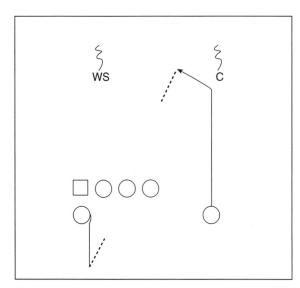

Post route in seam

■ Seam Post

On this route it is important that the receiver takes a good presnap look and reads the coverage as he comes off the line and hits the seam on his break. The quarterback must fire the ball, putting it on the receiver. He must not stretch him out or throw late, as that could result in an interception.

■ Deep Post

In throwing the deep post, the quarterback must throw the ball with some loft so that the receiver can run under it. He must not hang the ball and allow the defender to recover and intercept it.

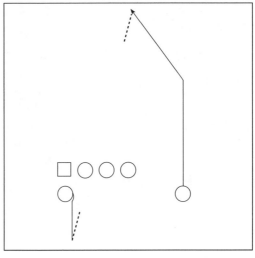

Deep post

■ In

On this route the quarterback must keep the ball down and not stretch the receiver out. The quarterback will find the lane and lead the ball to the receiver. The receiver could be called to sit out in the dead spot of the zone. If so, he will brake, turn his shoulder to the quarterback, and make eye contact. The quarterback will put the ball on the receiver.

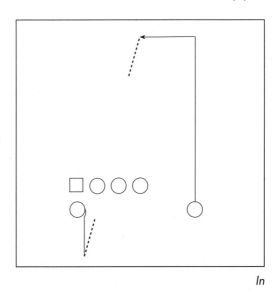

In

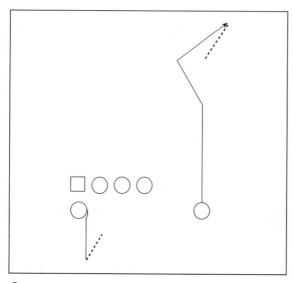

Corner

■ Corner

On the corner turn the quarterback needs to throw the ball to the outside of the receiver away from the defender. This allows the receiver to run to the ball and insures that if he can't get to it, the defender won't either. The ball must not hang because the defender will recover and battle the receiver for the catch.

Jim McMahon of BYU used the West Coast pass offense to set seven NCAA records. One of his favorite receivers was Glen Kozlowski, who ran the corner route to perfection.

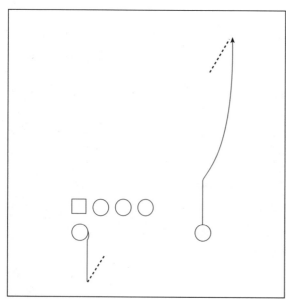

Takeoff

■ Takeoff

The takeoff route is a timing route, so the quarterback must set up and throw on time. He should throw over the receiver's inside shoulder with loft so that the receiver can run under it. The target should be a couple of yards inside the receiver so the pass ends up coming over the inside shoulder, but away from a safety moving over to play the ball.

Pass Protection

5

The passing game will only be as successful as the team is successful in protecting and giving the quarterback time to make his reads and throw the football downfield. This pass protection comes primarily from the offensive line. The running backs also have protection responsibility before they release into their pass routes, and the tight end may be used in pass protection if the quarterback wants total protection on a defensive back blitz.

Offensive Lineman Fundamentals

The success of any passing attack depends on the ability of the offensive line to give the quarterback time to find the open receivers and complete the passes. It takes time to develop the skill necessary to be a pass protector just as it takes time to develop skill in passing or catching the football. Each individual on the offensive line has a responsibility to perform, and in order to pass protect he also must be able to work as a unit with the player next to him. The offensive center must be strong and intelligent. He is responsible for recognizing defenses and calling the line blocking. The guards and tackles must be able to work together and communicate to pick up the defensive blitzes and protect the quarterback.

The offensive center is responsible for recognizing defenses and calling the line blocking.

The straight dropback pass is the most effective pass, because it allows the quarterback to read the whole field. The offensive linemen must be able to protect for the dropback pass to give the quarterback time to make these reads. This type of pass protection is referred to as a *pocket protection* (see figure 5.1).

The quarterback has the responsibility to get depth on his drop. This is a five- or seven-step drop that will let the quarterback set up behind his offensive line at about 5 to 7 yards. The guards and centers drop back about a yard off

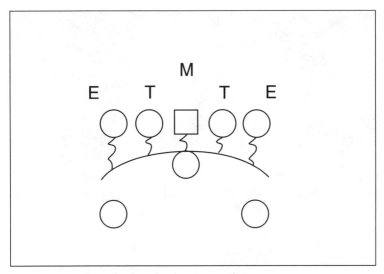

FIGURE 5.1 *Straight drop back pass, pocket protection*

the line of scrimmage and take a stand. The tackles drop a little deeper and force the defender around them to the outside.
The quarterback is instructed to step up in the pocket and
throw the football, because he is not going to be protected if
he leaves the pocket.

The offensive lineman is asked to do something that is
unnatural to a football player—to be patient and wait until the
defensive lineman makes his move and only engage a defensive
man if he comes into his area. This insures that there are no
gaps in the protection and the quarterback has time to throw.
The goal of pass protection is to give the quarterback four sec-
onds to throw the football. The lineman must take pride in the
job to be done and set a goal that no one touches the quarterback. The only way a passing game can be effective is to get
this type of performance from the offensive line.

Stance

The stance is the proper alignment of a player's body to start
each play. Before the snap offensive linemen should be positioned in a three-point stance. Tackles, guards, and centers
should place their feet shoulder-width apart, in a heel-instep
relationship, with the dominant foot back. Each lineman

Pass protection by the offensive line allows Steve Young time to scan for the open receiver.

should put very little weight on the down hand to allow for
quick forward, backward, and lateral movement. He should
place his arm loosely across his thigh. His back should be kept
straight, with the head up to see defenders across the line of
scrimmage. This position is the strongest and safest for the
back and neck.

Initial Move and Setup

The initial move and setup technique is extremely important in
pass blocking. The lineman must set up quickly, stepping back
away from the line of scrimmage or laterally if the defensive
man is aligned outside. The depth behind the line of scrimmage
should vary with the pass action called and the opponent's
defensive front alignment. The offensive lineman pushes up
into a two-point stance with his down hand. This projects the
offensive lineman into a position with his head up, eyes open
wide, back straight, rear end down, hands and arms up, and feet
positioned to move back or laterally in a split second.

Body Position

The lineman must position himself between the quarterback and the defensive pass rusher by backing off. He keeps his head up, rear end down, and back straight. He places his feet shoulder-width apart, keeps them moving, and flexes his knees. The weight of his body and head is over his feet, never in front of them. He holds his elbows in with the hands, ready to ward off the challenge of the defensive lineman.

Punch

Delivering a blow to stop the charge of the defensive lineman takes good timing. The player must let the defensive lineman get as close as 6 inches before delivering the blow to stop the charge. He must then step back away from the defensive lineman and recoil. The player must deliver the punch with his elbows locked and in close to the rib cage, rolling his wrists to get power. No, we aren't recommending that you teach your linemen to throw left hooks at charging defenders. Their hands and arms must stay within the planes of the shoulders.

Patience

An offensive lineman must be the protector and not the aggressor, and patience may be the hardest thing to teach him. He must keep his legs under him and always remain in a good blocking position even after delivering the punch. Linemen must be instructed to keep their rear ends down and their knees bent at all times.

Footwork

The most important skill for an offensive lineman is the ability to move his feet. The correct foot movement is a shuffle, with the player keeping one foot in contact with the ground at all times. Linemen should never cross their feet and should keep their bodies parallel to the line of scrimmage with their backs to the quarterback at all times.

Running Back Pass Protection

The running backs are an integral part of pass protection. The theory behind throwing the football from the dropback series is that the quarterback knows that if the defensive team brings seven rushers in any combination he is protected. This is because the five offensive linemen pick up five rushers and the two running backs pick up the other two rushers. The running back is responsible for blocking his defender just as the offensive lineman is responsible for blocking his defender.

Protecting Against the Inside Rush

The running back must set up by stepping up with his inside foot, and following with the outside foot ending up in a parallel position. His knees are flexed, back straight, head up, and elbows flexed and close to the sides of the body. His hands are up in front and slightly away from the chest and his eyes are on the onrushing defender.

The back meets the rusher, aggressively catches him, and drives him down inside away from the quarterback. The force comes from his legs but he hits with his hands and presses out with his arms. The inside hand stops the defender while the outside hand directs him inside. The back must not lunge forward, or he runs the risk of missing the rusher.

Protecting Against the Outside Rush

The back is in his blocking position with his eyes on the defender's numbers. He makes contact in an aggressive catch manner, generating force from the legs and out through the arms and hands. He gets separation by pressing out with the arms while moving the feet and maintaining position on the rusher.

Team Techniques of Pass Protection

The key to successful pass protection is to keep the protection as simple as possible. The ideal way to protect is to make each offensive player responsible for a defensive player. Then you know which player broke down if there is a breakdown in the protection. This is possible to do when playing against an odd defense, but because of the loops and twists off the even defense, it becomes necessary to zone block also.

Protecting Against Odd Defense

To give you the basic team concept of pass protection, in figure 5.2 the basic man-for-man protection is shown against a 3-4 or odd defense. In this protection you will notice that the large linemen on offense are going against the large defensive lineman, and the running backs are blocking on defensive linebackers who are more their size. This can be called with a *Bob* call, which can mean *big on big* or *back on backer*, so

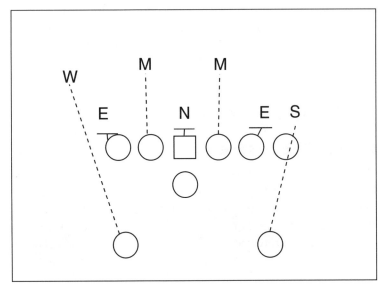

FIGURE 5.2 *Man-for-man pass protection*

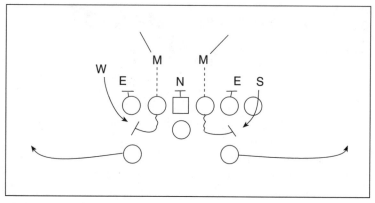

FIGURE 5.3 *Fan pass protection*

everyone knows whom to block. This protection holds up versus most odd defenses.

As we mentioned earlier, the success of the pro-style passing attack comes from getting five receivers into the pattern. The defense could prevent you from doing this by bringing their outside backers and dropping their inside backers according to the protection rule shown in figure 5.2. The offense must have an adjustment that they could make off the base protection to get the running back out into the pattern. This can be accomplished two ways. The first is an in-out read with the offensive guard. If the inside backer drops, the guard yells "Go!" to the running back and blocks the outside backer (see figure 5.3). This can be done on one or both sides according to how well your center blocks his man.

Slide Protection

Defenses are also lining a defensive end or a weakside linebacker outside on the weak side of the formation. A large defensive end rushing against a smaller back in our base protection can put quick pressure on the quarterback, so the second type of protection is the slide protection as illustrated in figure 5.4. Once again, this can be done on one or both sides.

Protecting Against Even Defense

The even defense can cause a man-to-man pass protection scheme problems, because when defenses loop or cross they may cause an offensive lineman to get screened off from his man, allowing one of the defensive players to come free. The most important rule of zone protection is to make your initial move back off the line of scrimmage and see what is happening in front of you. If the defensive man comes straight into you, block him just like it was man-to-man protection. If he goes down inside to the next lineman, you punch him and yell "Switch!" waiting for the looping lineman on a twist; then

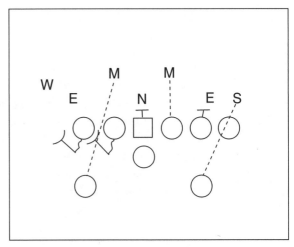

FIGURE 5.4 *Slide pass protection*

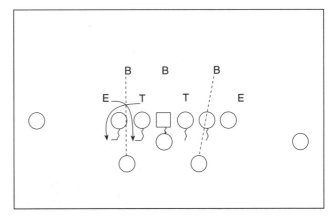

FIGURE 5.5 *Zone pass protection*

you pick him up. Figure 5.5 is an example. The key to success is for the linemen to talk to each other and not assume anything.

Protecting Against Safety Blitzes

The quarterback must be alert. As soon as he anticipates a safety blitz he must audibly tell the tight end to stay in and pass protect. The defense is now rushing eight players, but by keeping the tight end in to protect there are eight offensive players to protect the quarterback. The basic strong safety blitz can be picked up as shown in figure 5.6. The basic weak safety blitz can be picked up as shown in figure 5.7.

Pass protection requires much repetition so that the players know who to block against every defense. They must execute properly and be taught how to counter schemes and individual techniques. Much time needs to be spent with individual techniques and on blitz pickup run by a prep team from cards that are drawn up.

Offensive linemen do not get their names in the papers for scoring touchdowns, so they have to develop pride within. They get their recognition from knowing that, if the quarter-back does not get hit, the pro-style passing game will be suc-cessful and they will win as a unit.

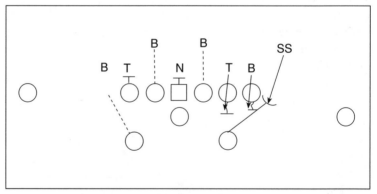

FIGURE 5.6 *Pass protection vs. strong safety blitz*

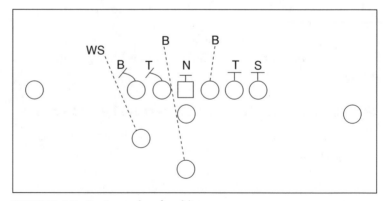

FIGURE 5.7 *Basic weak safety blitz*

Attacking Defensive Coverages

6

For the passing game to be effective, the quarterback must (1) know his attack thoroughly and understand where his receivers will be, and (2) know how to read and attack pass coverages. This enables him to find the open or single-coverage receiver and to use the audible system of changing plays at the line of scrimmage.

97

A presnap look can often reveal the defense's intentions.

Most coverages are revealed by alignment. Defenders will usually line up in position to effectively execute their assignments. A good presnap look can often reveal the defense's intentions. When taking the look, the quarterback should use the same routine, such as scanning the defense from one side to the other and back, down after down. This will keep the quarterback from looking directly at the point of attack. As he views the secondary, he notes the position, stance, and depth of alignment of the secondary defenders.

Secondary Coverages

■ Two-Deep Coverages Rotating Into Three-Deep Coverages

There are coaches who will have their secondary defenders line up in a two-deep zone or four-across-the-board look and then rotate when there is a pass. In this case the quarterback can use a post-snap read. On the snap of the ball he views down the center of

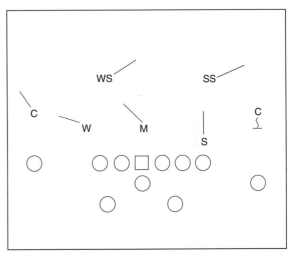

Two-deep look rotating into three-deep coverage

the defense or "through the goalpost" to see if the safeties remain in two-deep or rotate with one safety going to middle third coverage.

■ Pure Three-Deep Zone

This coverage will have the cornerbacks on the wide receivers with the safety lined up in the middle deeper than the corner-backs. The cornerbacks can line up in a position inside the wide receivers. This coverage is a favorite with teams using an eight-man front.

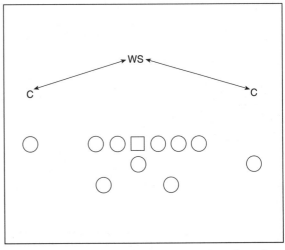

Pure three-deep

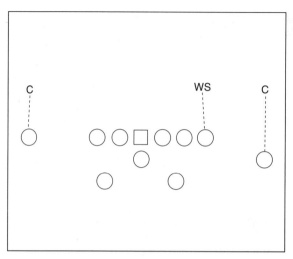

Man coverage

■ Man Coverage

When the safety lines up on the tight end, the quarterback is alerted to man coverage with linebacker dog (linebacker shooting in on rush). The cornerbacks will take an inside shade to stop the slant and other inside or crossing routes. Again, this coverage is associated with the eight-man front.

When presnap reading a four-deep secondary alignment, the quarterback checks the position and depth of the cornerbacks and safeties. The position of the strong safety is especially important in revealing the coverage.

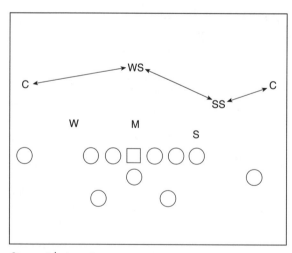

Strongside invert zone

■ Strongside Invert Zone

In this coverage, the strong safety lines up outside and closer to the line of scrimmage than the cornerbacks. The weak safety lines up deep and over the middle of the formation. On a dropback pass the strong safety goes to the flat, while the cornerbacks and weak safety play deep thirds. The strong safety and linebackers provide four short undercoverage men. This zone is popular with teams that want strongside zone rotation (to the two-receiver side) versus the pass and want to force the end run with the strong safety.

■ **Strongside Roll Zone**

This coverage has the strongside cornerback up closer toward the line of scrimmage. The strong safety is deeper and to the outside. The weak safety and weakside cornerback are at the same depth as the strong safety. This zone coverage is popular with teams who want to double-team the flanker on a pass and force the end run with

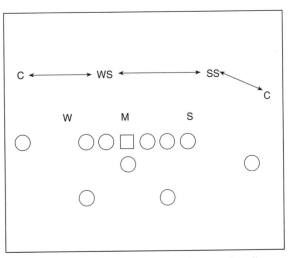

Strongside roll zone

the strongside cornerback. On a dropback pass the strongside corner rotates up and bumps the flanker inside, with the strong safety picking him up deep.

■ **Weakside Roll Zone**

In this coverage the weakside cornerback is up while the weak safety, strong safety, and strongside cornerback are at the same depth. The strong safety's vertical position is noticeably tighter to the tight end. Upon the recognition of dropback pass, the weakside cornerback rotates up to the weakside flat, bumping the split end to the inside

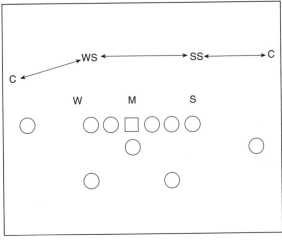

Weakside roll zone

while the cornerback picks him up deep. This coverage is effective when strategy calls for the split end to be double-teamed.

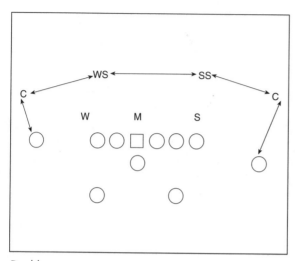

Double zone

■ Double Zone

This coverage has five defenders in the undercoverage with two safeties playing deep halves. The presnap look will be at the safeties back in their deep half position, while the cornerbacks are up in an outside alignment on the wide receivers. The cornerbacks look inside to determine run or pass. The wideouts are double-teamed on routes downfield, with the cornerbacks bumping them inside and the safeties picking them up deep. This can be an effective coverage for the intermediate pass when the undercoverage drops back 12 to 15 yards. It also permits the defense to play the end run with a corner force.

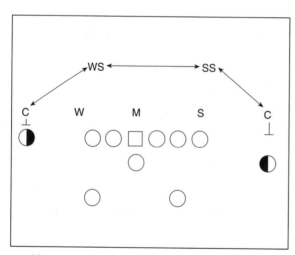

Double zone with man coverage underneath

■ Double Zone With Man Coverage Underneath

This coverage looks the same as double zone except that the cornerbacks are up tight on the wide receivers in bump-and-run position. The cornerbacks will usually take an inside shade on the wide receiver. Double man coverage, as this defense is called, enables the defense to play tight man-to-man coverage while allowing the two safeties to play deep half zones.

■ Man Coverage With Free Safety

This coverage has the cornerback lining up in an outside shade on the wide receivers. The strong safety is tight to the tight end at the same depth as the cornerbacks. The weak safety lines up deep over the middle to take away the deep post.

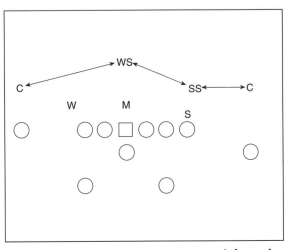

Man coverage with free safety

■ Four-Across-the-Board

When the quarterback sees the defensive backs lined up four-across at the same depth, he thinks man coverage with linebacker dog. The position of the weak safety lining up to pick up the halfback coming out of his route to the weakside allows a linebacker or linebackers to shoot in on the quarterback.

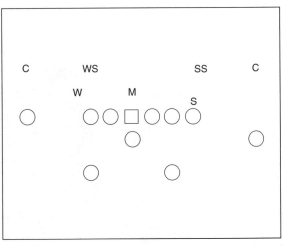

Four-across-the-board

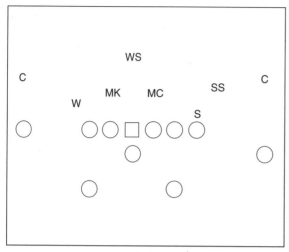

Strongside invert zone with five-underneath coverage

■ Strongside Invert Zone With Five-Underneath Coverage

This coverage looks like the strongside invert zone except the defense has the strongside outside linebackers dropping off into the seam between the hook and flat zones. The offense can read this as invert zone and call routes to attack the added coverage.

In the West Coast offense, consistent short passing gains are as welcome as the long bombs.

Attacking Coverages

The next step is knowing how to attack a coverage intelligently. The quarterback must know the strengths and weaknesses of a particular coverage and what kinds of plays work against it.

Pure Three-Deep Zone

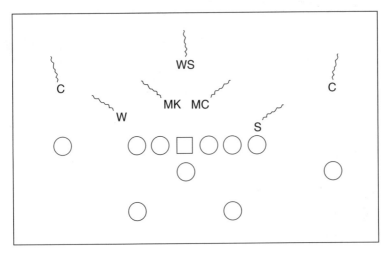

The pure three-deep zone has three deep zone defenders with four short zone defenders.

Attack

1. Horizontal or vertical stretch plays
2. Sideline floods
3. Turn-in route
4. Delays versus deep-dropping undercoverage
5. Out route to the soft corner on either side
6. Pass plays from Green formation
7. Motion to stretch zone coverage

Three-Deep Man Coverage

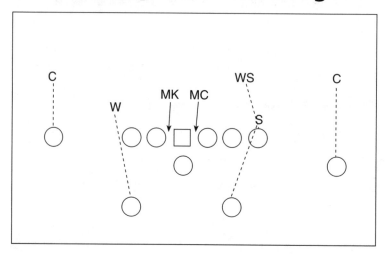

In the three-deep man coverage alignment, the quarterback can expect linebacker dogs, so the hot receiver principle or maximum protection with the tight end staying in for pass protection must be used.

Attack

1. Slant route by wide receivers; wide receiver motion across formation
2. Individual routes by wide receivers while using maximum protection scheme
3. Back out weakside HB option route
4. Takeoff routes
5. Crossing routes; shallow cross
6. Hot receiver scheme
7. Green formation to spread out secondary

Man-to-Man With Free Safety

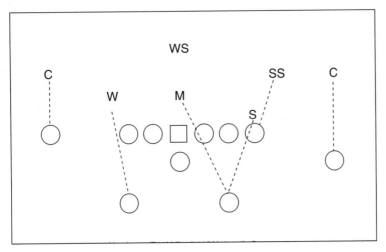

This coverage allows tight man coverage with the free safety helping deep. Corners will line up in an outside shade, knowing that the free safety will play deep middle. This can be effective in defending the post out routes and delay routes. The linebackers are man-to-man on the backs.

Attack

1. Vertical stretch
2. Crossing routes; shallow cross; motion to clear out under-coverage
3. Post corner
4. Throw to backs isolated on backers
5. Send a receiver down through the weak safety to occupy him, leaving other defenders one-on-one
6. Play-action passes
7. Pick type or rub passes

Four-Short, Three-Deep Invert Zone

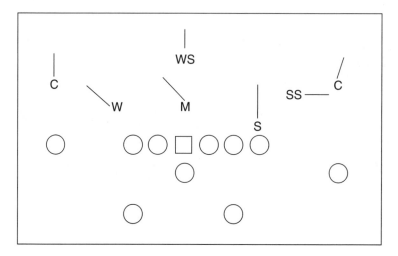

This coverage is the standard zone coverage, featuring four defenders covering short with three covering deep. Having the strong safety covering the strongside flat allows him to be the forceman to any end run to his side. The defense could rotate weak with the weak safety going to the flat and the strong safety to deep middle, but most teams will rotate strongside.

Attack

1. Vertical stretch
2. Horizontal stretch (turn-in and out routes)
3. Attack seams in undercoverage
4. Delay routes
5. Option routes
6. Motion to stretch zone coverage
7. Quick out or speed out to weakside

Roll Coverage

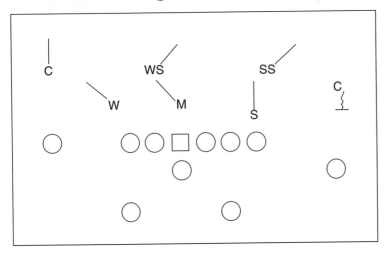

Roll coverage is still basically a four-short, three-deep zone. The important point is that to the side of the roll a cornerback will play short, while a safety will play deep behind the cornerback. For that reason many teams like to throw away from rotation when throwing the speed out route.

Attack

1. Vertical stretch
2. Horizontal stretch; motion to stretch zone
3. Out route away from rotation
4. Delay routes
5. Option routes

Two-Deep, Five-Under Zone

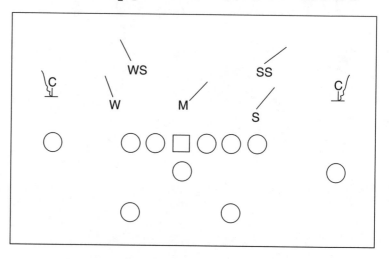

This coverage is popular versus the short to intermediate passing attack, since there are five defenders across the field in undercoverage. The cornerbacks will try to funnel the wide receivers inside where there is help. The two safeties play the deep halves. This is a popular coverage for teams using reduce type defensive alignments.

Attack

1. Vertical stretch
2. Fade and corner routes with tight end down the middle
3. Delay routes; shallow cross
4. Motion to stretch zone coverage
5. Horizontal stretch on deep safeties forcing two to cover three-deep zones

Double Zone With Man
Coverage Underneath

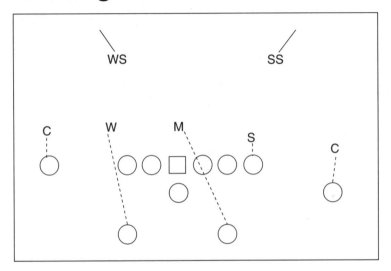

The safeties line up as in double zone but the undercoverage now covers man-to-man. The corners line up in a press technique using an inside shade to help defense crossing routes.

Attack

1. Vertical stretch
2. Crossing routes; motion to clear out undercoverage
3. Pick type or rub passes
4. Corner routes with tight end running post
5. Throw to backs
6. Option routes

Prevent Coverage

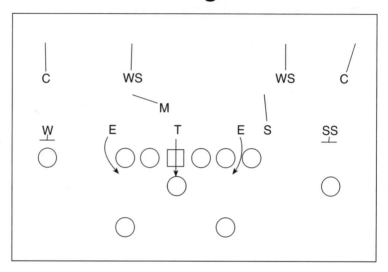

This coverage is used in sure passing situations, especially during the last two minutes of the fourth quarter. The defense is set to take away the deep pass first and, secondly, to keep all other passes in front of the coverage.

Attack

1. Three-level sideline flood (vertical stretch)
2. Crossing routes
3. Sideline routes
4. Screen and possibly draw
5. Two receivers deep to a side with inside receiver occupying the safety while the outside receiver goes one-on-one with the corner

Controlling the Safety Blitz With the Sight Adjustment

There are times when the defense will send a safety in on blitz. The offense can counteract this by using the sight adjustment. The sight adjustment involves the quarterback and the two wide receivers. It does not apply to called runs, play-action passes, or any three-step drop passes.

In executing this maneuver, when a wide receiver sees the safety to his side shoot, he breaks into a slant route expecting the ball immediately. Versus bump-and-run, he runs a fade route. If the safety fakes the blitz and drops back into coverage, the wide receiver runs his called route. See figures 6.1 and 6.2.

The backs use their presnap look to alert them to the safety blitz. They will be responsible for the most dangerous inside rushes. If there is no blitz, they will execute their base assignment.

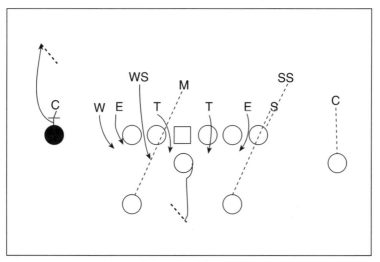

FIGURE 6.1 *WS blitz with bump-and-run coverage*

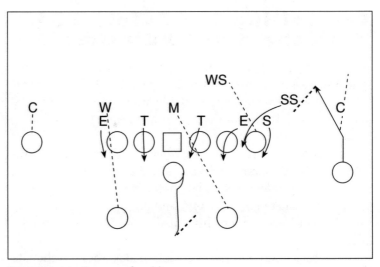

FIGURE 6.2 *Strong safety blitz*

Twenty Great Passing Plays

The 20 plays presented in this playbook have been used with great success by college teams such as Brigham Young University and pro teams such as the San Francisco 49ers and the Green Bay Packers. The plays are diagrammed and explained, and assignments for the offensive players are presented. To help you execute the plays effectively, they're diagrammed against all the defensive coverages discussed in chapter 6. Play-action passing plays are presented at the end of the playbook. Use this playbook to put points on the scoreboard and win with the passing game.

Quick Out

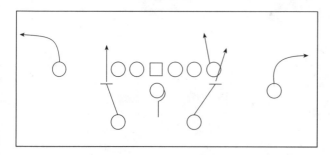

This play is effective versus loose corner coverage. It is a timing route and if the ball is thrown late or hangs, it will be intercepted. If thrown properly the result is a 5- to 7-yard gain or more. Versus bump-and-run coverage, the receiver can fade or run the out, letting the defender push him toward the sideline.

Assignments

Split end: Quick out; normal to minimum split; on break, snap head around for the ball

Tight end: Pop route; regular split; take inside release and look for the ball

Flanker: Quick out; normal to minimum split; on break, snap head around for the ball

Fullback: Drive on end man; block on line; run close route

Halfback: Drive on end man; block on line; run close route

Quarterback: Presnap look for softest corner; work softest corner; three steps and throw; do not throw late or hang the ball

Versus Various Defenses

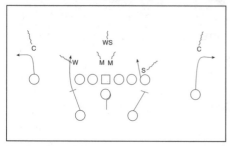

Versus three-deep

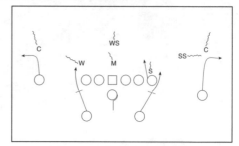

Versus four-short, three-deep (invert)

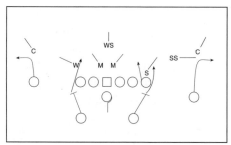

Versus invert three-deep

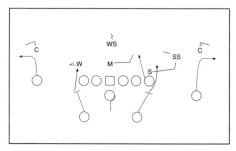

Versus man

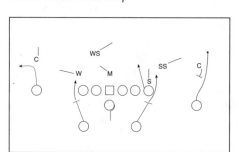

Versus roll strong

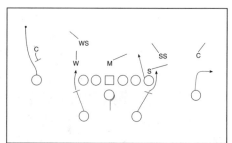

Versus roll weak

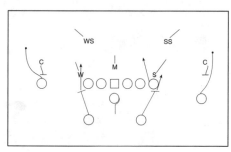

Versus double zone

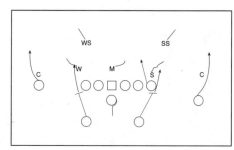

Versus double man

Slant

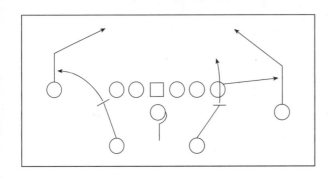

The slant play is effective versus man coverage, three-deep zone, a strong safety that lines up loose on the tight end, blitz, and when the corners are outside-conscious. This is a timing play in which the quarterback must hit the receiver in stride, not stretching him out and not throwing late. As with all three-step drop plays, the line will block aggressively with a quick set to keep defensive hands down.

Assignments

Split end: Slant route; maximum split; run aggressively

Tight end: Straight route; look for ball on release

Flanker: Slant route; maximum split; run aggressively

Fullback: Drive on end man; block on line; run close route

Halfback: Drive on end man; block on line; run shallow shoot

Quarterback: Presnap look for best side; three steps and throw; strongside work Y to Z, weakside work X to HB; don't stretch the receiver out

Versus Various Defenses

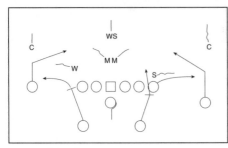

Versus three-deep

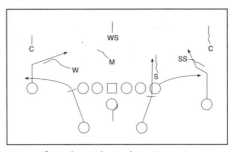

Versus four-short, three-deep (invert)

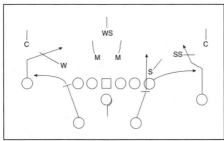

Versus Invert three-deep

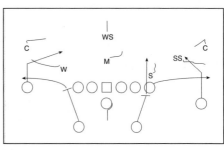

Versus man

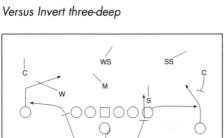

Versus roll strong

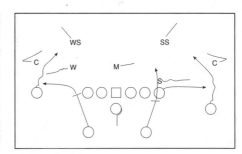

Versus roll weak

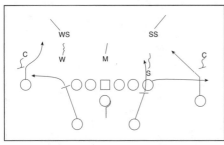

Versus double zone

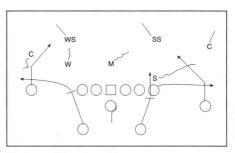

Versus double man

Tight End Option

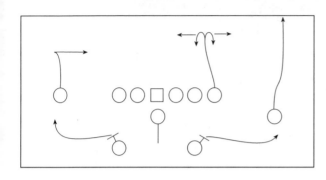

This play, a good ball-control pass, is effective against man or zone coverage. The emphasis is on the tight end and split end reading the coverage and adjusting their routes to get open. The tight end hooks up versus zone. Versus man coverage, he breaks away from coverage. When he and the quarterback make eye contact, the ball is thrown.

Assignments

Split end: Smash route; maximum split; read coverage; make eye contact with the quarterback for ball

Tight end: Release inside and get upfield; hug nearest defender and read coverage; at 8- to 10-yard depth make move; hook up versus zone, break away from man coverage; make eye contact with quarterback when you want the ball; versus zone, get upfield and break to open area, don't simply release to area

Flanker: Takeoff; maximum split

Fullback: Check; swing route

Halfback: Check; swing route

Quarterback: Presnap look; read tight end coverage as you take five-step drop; when tight end makes eye contact, deliver the ball if he's open; otherwise, look to X on smash route

Versus Various Defenses

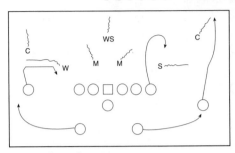

Versus three-deep

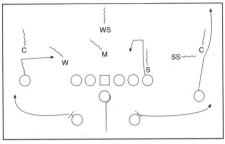

Versus four-short, three-deep (invert)

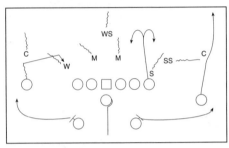

Versus invert three-deep

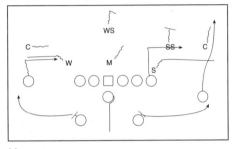

Versus man

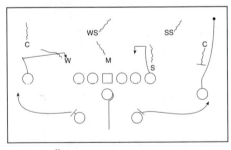

Versus roll strong

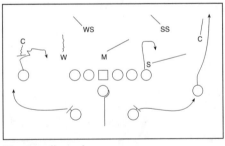

Versus roll weak

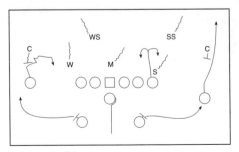

Versus double zone

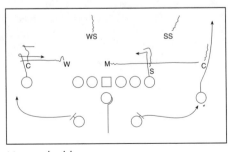

Versus double man

Halfback Option

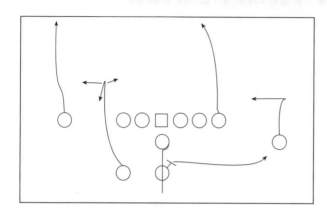

This play has the halfback releasing immediately out on route. He reads the coverage as he releases. Versus dog or blitz, he runs a shallow shoot to the flat, looking for the ball to come quickly. Otherwise he hooks up versus zone or breaks away from the defender against man coverage. This is a good ball-control pass play. The flanker, running a smash route, is the secondary receiver.

Assignments

Split end: Takeoff; maximum split

Tight end: Post; clear out WS

Flanker: Smash route; maximum split; read coverage; make eye contact with quarterback for the ball

Fullback: Check; swing route

Halfback: Option route; release upfield 6 to 8 yards, reading coverage; run shallow shoot versus dog or blitz; versus zone break to open area and hook up; versus man coverage break away from defender; establish eye contact with quarterback for the ball

Quarterback: Presnap look; read HB coverage as you take your five-step drop; if HB open, deliver ball when he makes eye contact with you; if not open, go to flanker on smash route

Versus Various Defenses

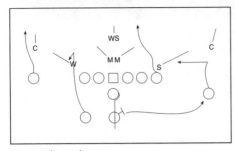

Versus three-deep

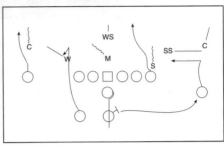

Versus four-short, three-deep (invert)

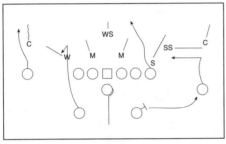

Versus invert three-deep

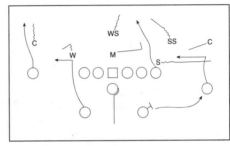

Versus man

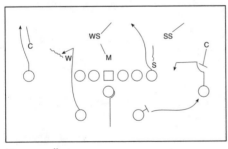

Versus roll strong

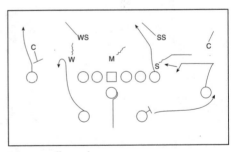

Versus roll weak

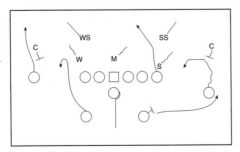

Versus double zone

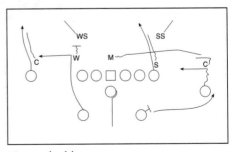

Versus double man

Fullback Option
(80 Series)

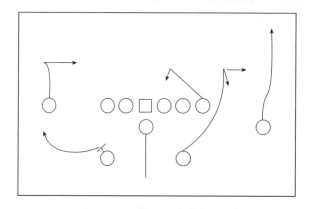

This play has the fullback immediately releasing out on route and reading the coverage. Versus strongside dog or blitz, the fullback runs a shallow shoot route and looks for the ball immediately. Otherwise, he hooks up versus zone and breaks away from the defender versus man coverage.

Assignments

Split end: Smash route; maximum split

Tight end: Pop hook; control inside coverage; work away from defender

Flanker: Takeoff; maximum split

Fullback: Option route; read coverage and adjust route; make eye contact with quarterback for ball

Halfback: Check; swing route

Quarterback: Presnap look; five-step drop; read coverage and work FB to Y to X

Versus Various Defenses

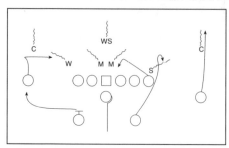

Versus three-deep

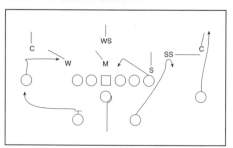

Versus four-short, three-deep (invert)

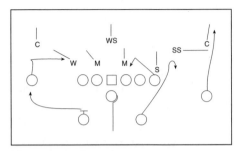

Versus invert three-deep

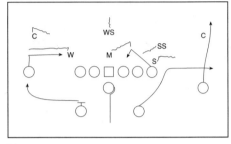

Versus man

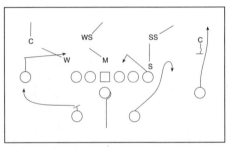

Versus roll strong

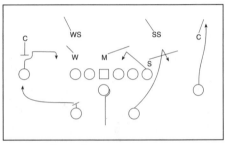

Versus roll weak

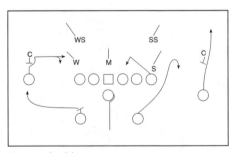

Versus double zone

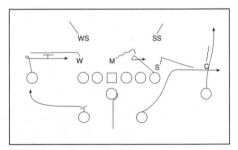

Versus double man

Turn-In

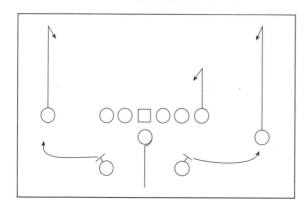

This play attacks the field and is good against any four-short, three-deep zone. It can also be effective versus man coverage when receivers sell the take-off route and break back to the quarterback. The backs swinging out wide become effective receivers when the undercoverage drops to shut off the turn-in routes.

Assignments

Split end: Turn-in route; maximum split; threaten the defender deep; come back for ball; versus bump-and-run, get defender running downfield, come back quickly for ball as he overruns

Tight end: Turn-in route; inside release; get upfield and find hole in coverage

Flanker: Turn-in route; maximum split; threaten the defender deep; come back for ball; versus bump-and-run, get defender running downfield and break back for ball as he overruns

Fullback: Check; swing route

Halfback: Check; swing route

Quarterback: Presnap look; five-step drop if turn-in is at 12 yards; seven-step drop if route is at 14 yards; key Mike backer to WS; if either one goes hard weakside, throw strongside, Y to Z to FB; if both stay middle, throw weakside, X to HB to Y; keep the ball down on turn-in route ; undercoverage drops to turn-in hit swing route, keeping the ball in front of the back

Versus Various Defenses

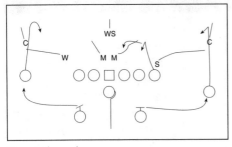

Versus three-deep

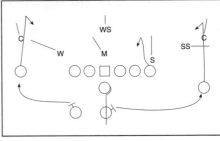

Versus four-short, three-deep (invert)

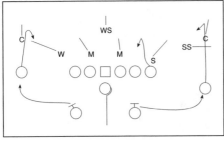

Versus invert three-deep

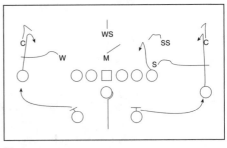

Versus man

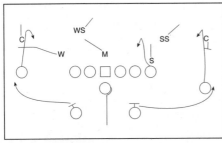

Versus roll strong

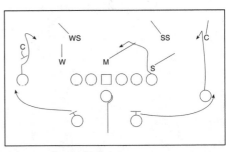

Versus roll weak

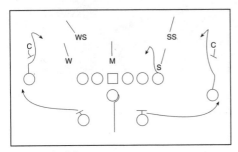

Versus double zone

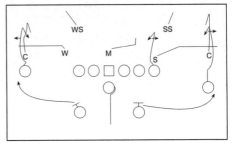

Versus double man

Turn-In Route From Slot
(Orange)

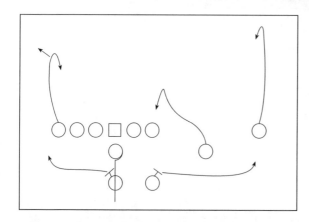

Running the turn-in play from slot allows the offense to find holes in the coverage from different points of release. This formation puts both wide receivers to one side, allowing the flanker to find the hole over the middle.

Assignments

Split end: Turn in; maximum split; work back to quarterback; versus bump-and-run, break straight back to quarterback, be ready to work outside for ball

Tight end: Turn in; release outside and upfield; run corner route versus roll coverage to your side

Flanker: Inside release; run turn-in to the inside; versus dog, expect quick pass; versus bump-and-run, break straight back to quarterback

Fullback: Check; swing route

Halfback: Check; swing route

Quarterback: Presnap look; 5 or 7 step drop; key Mike to WS; both stay middle, work Y1 to F2; either one goes hard strong (TE side), throws weak; Z1 to X2 to H3.

Versus Various Defenses

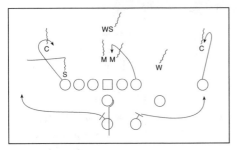

Versus three-deep

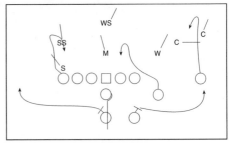

Versus four-short, three-deep (invert)

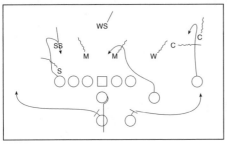

Versus invert three-deep

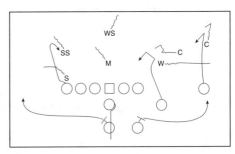

Versus man

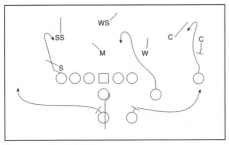

Versus roll weak

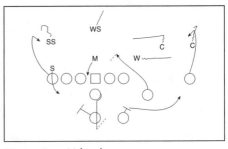

Versus Sam-Mike dog

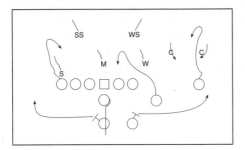

Versus double zone

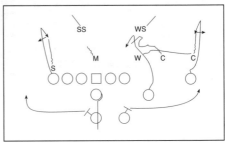

Versus double man

Speed Out

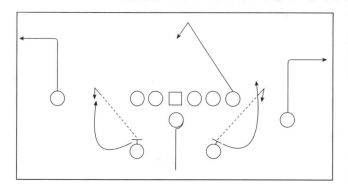

The speed out play is good against any four-short, three-deep zone or man coverage. Corners that line up loose on receivers or are inside-conscious are vulnerable. The route can also be effective versus man and two-deep coverages if the quarterback can hit the fade route consistently.

Assignments

Split end: Speed out route; minimum to normal split; threaten deep; get head around on break; versus roll-up corner or bump-and-run, run fade route

Tight end: Hook route; inside release and get upfield; versus two-deep, break on post route

Flanker: Same as split end

Fullback: Check; stop or seam route

Halfback: Check; stop or seam route

Quarterback: Five-step drop; presnap look for the best-located safety (the safety that lines up farthest from a wide receiver); work outside-in to that side; versus two-deep, key the strong safety; SS off the hash, hit Y, SS on the hash, hit Z; a major key to the success of this route is *timing*; the QB must set up quickly and get the ball off to the receiver

Versus Various Defenses

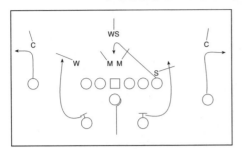

Versus three-deep

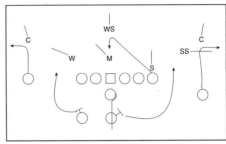

Versus four-short, three-deep (invert)

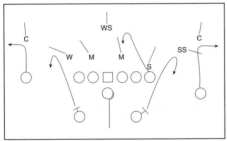

Versus invert three-deep

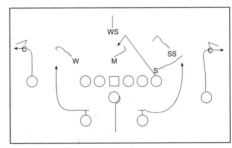

Versus man

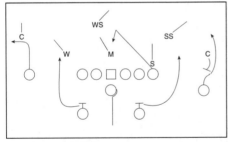

Versus roll strong

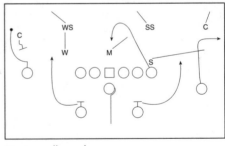

Versus roll weak

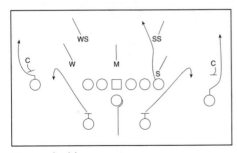

Versus double zone

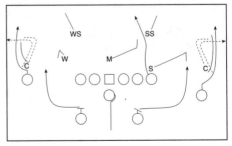

Versus double man

Corner

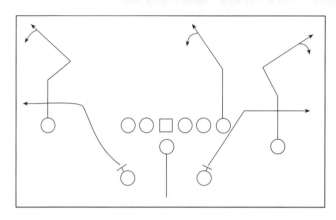

The corner route is most effective versus two-deep man or zone and conventional man-for-man coverage. The key to running this route effectively is to sell the post, then break to the corner to get separation from the defender.

Assignments

Split end: Post corner route; normal split; sell the post and break to the corner; versus a cornerback that lays back deep, adjust to sideline; versus bump-and-run, bend defender to inside on post move and break to corner; versus roll-up cornerback, release inside, get upfield, maintain width, and break to corner

Tight end: Post route; versus safety playing deep middle, adjust to deep turn-in

Flanker: Same as split end

Fullback: Check; flat route at 6 to 8 yards

Halfback: Check; flat route at 6 to 8 yards

Quarterback: Seven-step drop; scan right to left; throw to outside so receiver can run to ball; aware of down and distance for use of backs

Versus Various Defenses

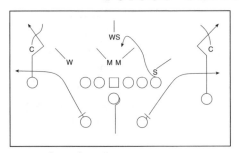

Versus three-deep

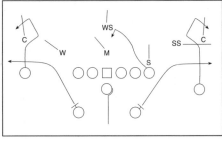

Versus four-short, three-deep (invert)

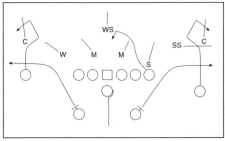

Versus invert three-deep

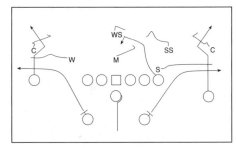

Versus man

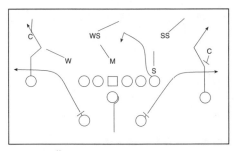

Versus roll strong

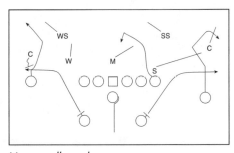

Versus roll weak

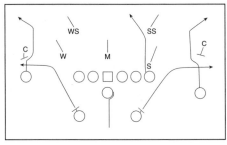

Versus double zone

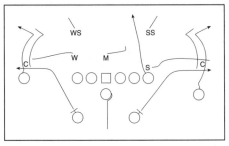

Versus double man

Tight End Bench

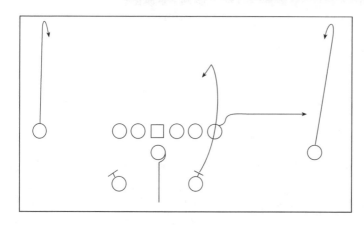

This play is effective attacking the strongside flat, man, or zone coverage. It can also be effective versus double man or double zone coverage.

Assignments

Split end: Turn-in; maximum split

Tight end: Bench; outside release; on break, look for ball

Flanker: Turn-in; maximum split

Fullback: Check; run close, hook route; hook up at 6 yards

Halfback: Block

Quarterback: Presnap look; five-step drop; read flat coverage, see strong safety and work Y1 to Z2 to F3

Versus Various Defenses

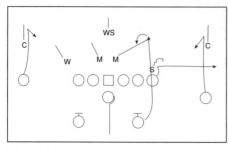

Versus three-deep

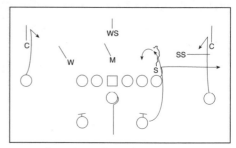

Versus four-short, three-deep (invert)

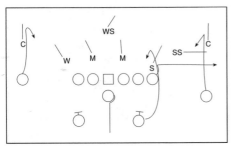

Versus invert three-deep

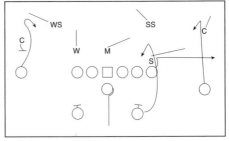

Versus man

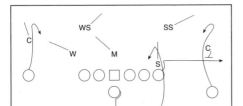

Versus roll strong

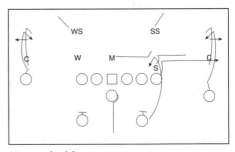

Versus roll weak

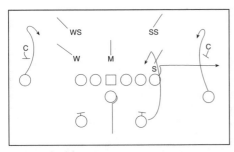

Versus double zone

Versus double man

Tight End Delay

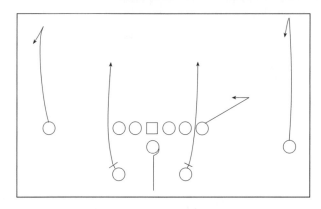

The tight end delay is most effective against zone coverage. It is especially effective versus deep-dropping undercoverage. Versus man coverage, the tight end must make an outside move and come back to the inside (see figure 7.1).

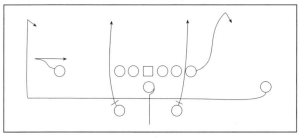

FIGURE 7.1 *Tight end delay versus man coverage (top) and deep-dropping undercoverage (bottom).*

Assignments

Split end: Comeback route at 15 yards; normal split

Tight end: Release outside and run delay route at 5 to 6 yards; don't rush route; allow fullback to clear out coverage, come underneath without gaining ground; versus man, make good fake and break inside; can execute this play with tight end blocking two counts and then releasing inside

Flanker: Turn-in; maximum split; flanker is dump-off receiver

Fullback: Check, release out on close route

Halfback: Check, release out on close route

Quarterback: Seven-step drop; look downfield to force undercoverage to drop; work Y1 to Z2; a variation can have split end in tightened-down split, flanker in motion across formation, and on snap, split end running delay route

Versus Various Defenses

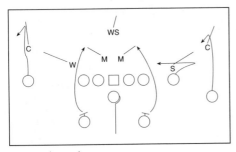

Versus three-deep

Versus four-short, three-deep (invert)

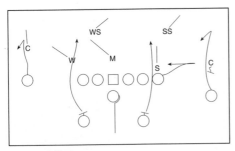

Versus invert three-deep

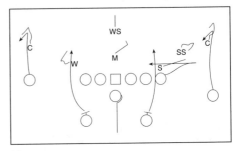

Versus man

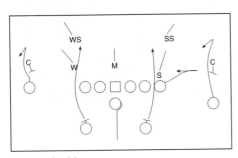

Versus roll strong

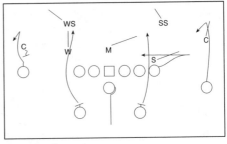

Versus roll weak

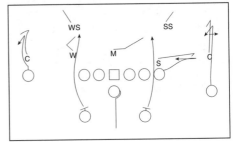

Versus double zone

Versus double man

Vertical Stretch

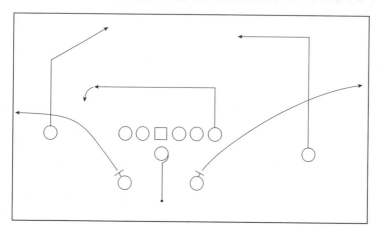

The vertical stretch is an all-purpose pattern effective against both man and zone coverage. Versus man coverage, receivers break and run from defenders. Versus zone the coverage is attacked on three levels. This is an effective pass in long-yardage situations.

Assignments

Split end: Normal split; run post route

Tight end: Regular split; run center route; get past linebackers; be prepared to hang in open area weakside

Flanker: Maximum split; run in route at 14 to 16 yards; do not gain ground when crossing field; versus zone, throttle down in open window or seam

Fullback: Check; release out on shoot route to 10 yards, hook up at sideline

Halfback: Check; run fan route

Quarterback: Presnap look; seven-step drop; key weak safety, read undercoverage; work X1 to Y2 to Z2; if safety takes away the post, work Y to Z; don't stretch out the flanker on the crossing route

An effective variation of this play has the flanker running a post across or dig route and the halfback running an angle route underneath the coverage (see figure 7.2). The post across hits the middle of the defense sooner than the in route. It is hard to defend if the receiver sells the post move and then breaks flat across the formation. As he comes across he will throttle down in the seams versus zone coverage. Having the halfback angle under the undercoverage takes advantage of deep-dropping undercoverage getting back to shut off the post across route. The progression of receivers for the quarterback changes to X1 to Z2 to HB3.

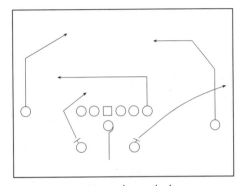

FIGURE 7.2 *Vertical stretch dig route*

The coach can have the wide receivers exchange assignments by calling the play and calling "Swap!" (see figure 7.3). When this term is used the split end runs the in route and the flanker, the post. The tight end releases upfield for 5 yards and comes over the formations, gaining depth to 10 yards. The progression of receivers is Z1 to Y2 to X3.

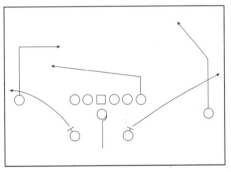

FIGURE 7.3 *"Swap" call*

Another adjustment that is excellent versus two-deep coverage and permits the offense to stretch the middle and weakside area is to send the tight end 5 to 8 yards deep across the field (see figure 7.4). Versus man coverage, he breaks away; versus zone, he will hang in the hole. The progression is X1 to Y2 to Z3.

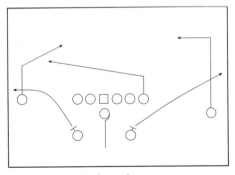

FIGURE 7.4 *Tight end over*

Versus Various Defenses

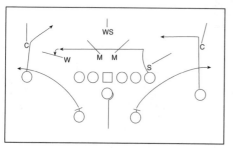

Versus three-deep

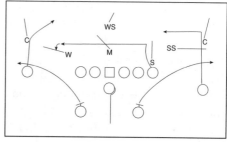

Versus four-short, three-deep (invert)

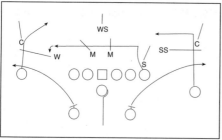

Versus invert three-deep

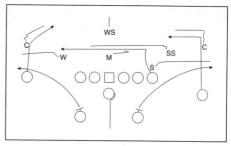

Versus man

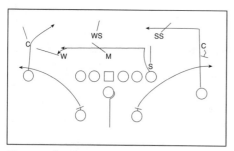

Versus roll strong

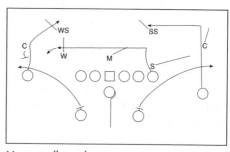

Versus roll weak

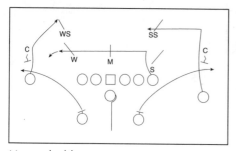

Versus double zone

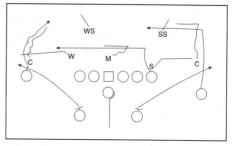

Versus double man

Strongside Flood

The strongside flood is part of the vertical stretch family, effective against both man and zone coverage. It features running routes versus man coverage, and three-level attack versus zone.

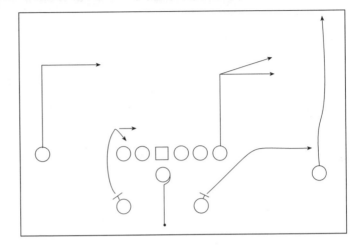

Assignments

Split end: Maximum split; run 14 to 16 yards in route; be aggressive coming inside

Tight end: Regular split; inside release, run drag route; drag versus man, sail route versus zone; sit out versus roll-up corner

Flanker: Maximum split; run takeoff route hard to clear it out; if ball is called to you, assume ball will be overthrown and be ready to run to it

Fullback: Check; run shoot route; be ready for ball

Halfback: Check; run cross route; run hook versus zone, cross versus man coverage

Quarterback: Seven-step drop; key strong safety, read flat coverage and work Y1 to F2 to X3; when looking for deep pass to flanker as first choice, work Z1 to Y2 to F3

Versus Various Defenses

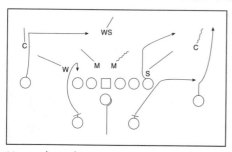

Versus three-deep

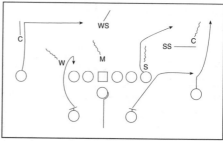

Versus four-short, three-deep (invert)

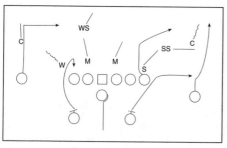

Versus invert three-deep

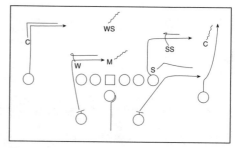

Versus man

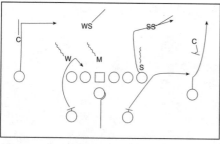

Versus roll strong

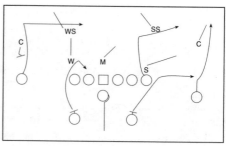

Versus roll weak

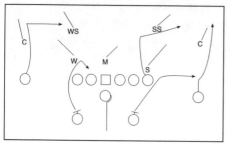

Versus double zone

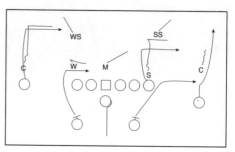

Versus double man

Shallow Route Plays

These plays take advantage of deep-dropping undercoverge and man-for-man defenses. By running receivers behind the undercoverage and a receiver shallow and in front, the coverage is stretched or cleared out. Because the receiver is running shallow across, he can immediately get separation from the

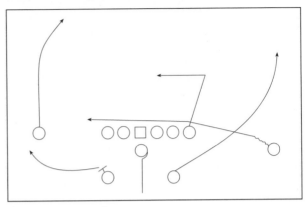

FIGURE 7.5 *Shallow cross*

defender covering man-to-man. The defender then must cover him across the field.

Shallow cross is also great versus dogging linebackers, since the pass is short and quick. The receiver is running away from the defender as he receives the ball. An example of this pass concept is the following pass play from the 80 series (see figure 7.5).

Assignments

Split end:	Post route; maximum split; clear it out deep
Tight end:	Middle route at 12 yards; inside release; read coverage; versus man coverage, break across, getting separation from defender; versus zone, look for hole to sit out and come straight back to ball
Flanker:	Zip motion; release behind TE; run shallow cross route; make eye contact with quarterback for ball; versus zone, sit out in weakside flat
Fullback:	Takeoff route; get width
Halfback:	Check; swing swing route
Quarterback:	Presnap look; five-step drop; read undercoverage and work Z1 to Y2 to FB3; play features a rubbing action between the tight end and flanker against man coverage

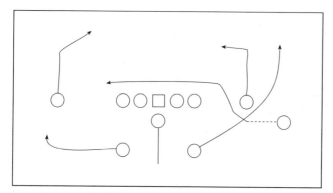

FIGURE 7.6 *Flanker inside on motion*

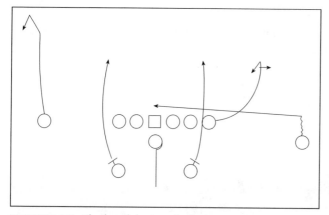

FIGURE 7.7 *Flanker delaying shallow cross*

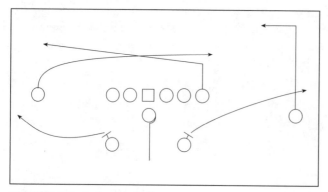

FIGURE 7.8 *Split end shallow cross*

Another variation of this concept has the tight end flex his split, bringing the flanker inside on motion (see figure 7.6). The offense can attack by running the tight end delay pass play, except exchanging the assignments of the tight end and flanker. The tight end runs his stop hook route while the flanker delays and comes underneath (see figure 7.7). The same idea could be run with the split end releasing underneath the crossing tight end (see figure 7.8).

Versus Various Defenses

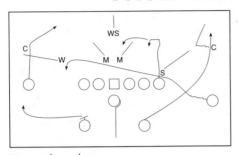

Versus three-deep

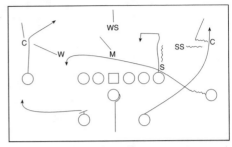

Versus four-short, three-deep (invert)

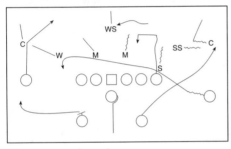

Versus invert three-deep

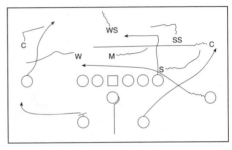

Versus man

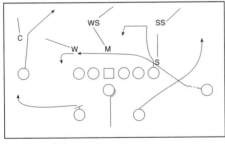

Versus roll strong

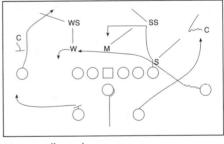

Versus roll weak

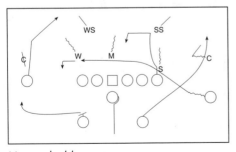

Versus double zone

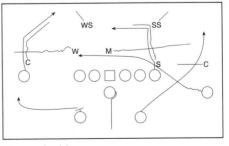

Versus double man

Post Vertical Stretch

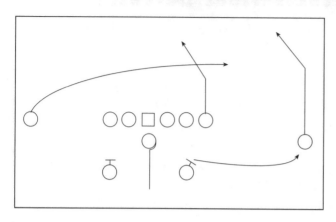

This pass play attacks three levels. By coming over, the split end can break away from man coverage. The tight end can occupy any middle third defenders, making one-on-one coverage for the flanker. The play is also effective versus two-deep coverage.

Assignments

Split end: Minimum or flex split; run across field, avoiding dropping linebackers, getting 15 to 18 yards in depth in the strongside flat

Tight end: Post route

Flanker: Post route; maximum split; hit seam

Fullback: Check; run shoot route, clear out flat coverage

Halfback: Block

Quarterback: Presnap look; seven-step drop; read strongside coverage and work Z1 to X2 to F3; versus two-deep work Y or Z1, then to X3

Versus Various Defenses

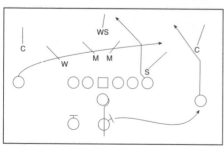

Versus three-deep

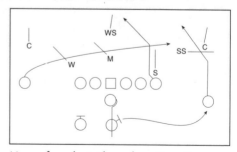

Versus four-short, three-deep (invert)

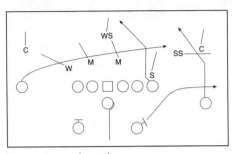

Versus invert three-deep

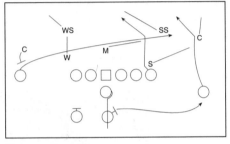

Versus man

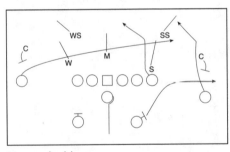

Versus roll strong

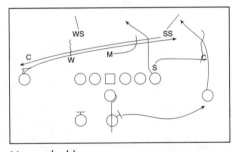

Versus roll weak

![double zone diagram]

Versus double zone

![double man diagram]

Versus double man

Weakside Flood
(Vertical Stretch)

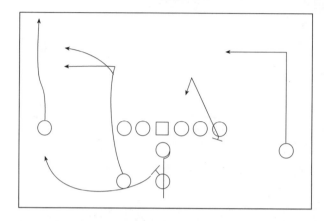

This pattern, part of the vertical stretch family, is effective against both man and zone coverage. It allows the offense to immediately release the halfback out on route to work against the weakside coverage.

Assignments

Split end: Maximum split; clear it out deep

Tight end: Slow block; block the rush; if no rush, hook up in open area over middle

Flanker: Maximum split; run in route at 14 to 16 yards versus zone, throttle down in open seam

Fullback: Check; run swing route, expect the ball

Halfback: Release immediately out on route; run corner versus zone; break to sideline on out versus man coverage

Quarterback: Key weakside linebacker and work H1 to F2 to Z3; can work X1 to H2 to F3 progression when looking for split end to be first choice; seven-step drop

The same kind of design can be run from Orange or Yellow formations. But because the two-receiver side could be defended as a strongside, the slot will adjust this route, just like the tight end would, against various coverages (see Figure 7.9).

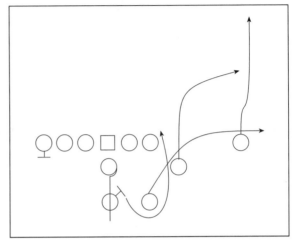

FIGURE 7.9 *Slot alignment*

Versus Various Defenses

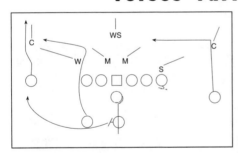

Versus three-deep

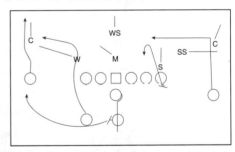

Versus four-short, three-deep (invert)

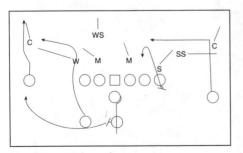

Versus invert three-deep

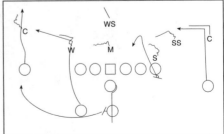

Versus man

Versus Various Defenses (cont.)

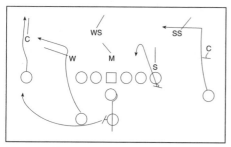

Versus roll strong

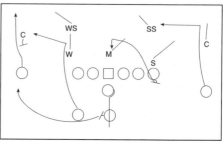

Versus roll weak

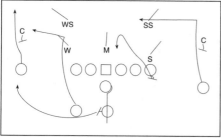

Versus double zone

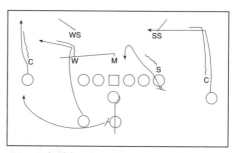

Versus double man

"If you can touch it you can catch it." Pass receptions are the key to making the West Coast offense work.

Smash Option (70 Series)

This option play attacks the weakside. It allows the split end to adjust his route versus man or zone coverage. It can have a pick action versus man coverage, is a good ball-control pass, and it can stretch weakside zone coverage.

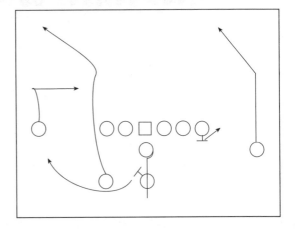

Assignments

Split end: Smash route; maximum split; versus weakside blitz (corner or safety) expect the ball

Tight end: Slow block, release outside

Flanker: Post route; normal split

Fullback: 70 protection; run swing route

Halfback: Release out on corner route

Quarterback: Seven-step drop; quarterback works H1 to X2 off the cornerback read; if weakside blitz, HB is the receiver; if strongside blitz, 2 is receiver on post

Versus Various Defenses

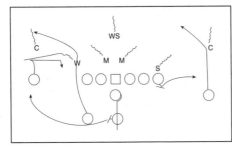

Versus three-deep

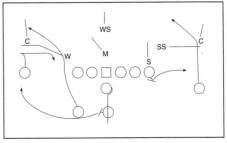

Versus four-short, three-deep (invert)

Versus Various Defenses (cont.)

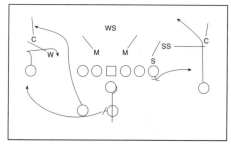

Versus invert three-deep

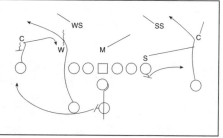

Versus man

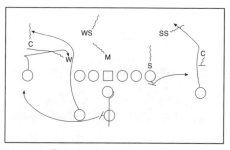

Versus roll strong

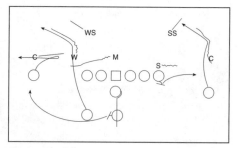

Versus roll weak

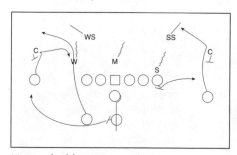

Versus double zone

Versus double man

Dash Pass

This pass concept is effective versus a hard-charging rush on drop-back action. It allows the quarterback to influence the rush upfield, rolls out getting width, and pull up for the throw.

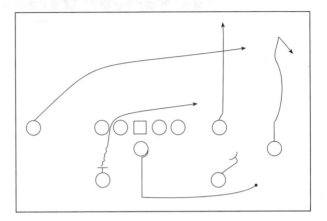

Assignments

Split end: Over route; normal split; get over to 20 to 25 yards depth

Tight end: Takeoff route; flex split to get outside backer to align outside with you; close it out deep; versus SS blitz run out route

Flanker: Deep comeback route; normal to maximum split; leave enough room outside to make the comeback move; versus SS blitz, run takeoff

Fullback: Check backer; help tackle, blocking outside in; stay high

Halfback: Check; release through on cross route

Quarterback: Presnap look; five-step drop, hesitate one count; roll out wide and pull up for throw; work Z1 to X2 to HB3

Versus Various Defenses

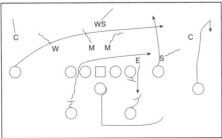

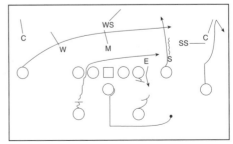

Versus three-deep

Versus four-short, three-deep (invert)

Versus Various Defenses (cont.)

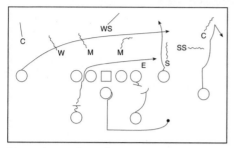

Versus Invert three-deep

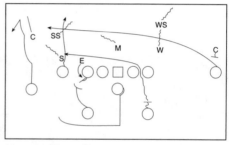

Versus man

Versus roll strong

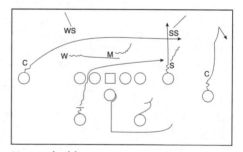

Versus roll weak

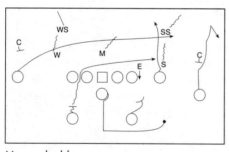

Versus double zone

Versus double man

70 Series With Halfback Motion

Putting the halfback in motion outside the wide receiver can stretch a zone or cause a man defender to lock onto the halfback. This maneuver can be used to reveal man or zone coverage. The split end will read the coverage and adjust his route

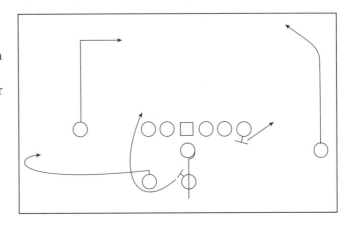

against man or zone. Versus zone, he will sit out in the seam; versus man, he will break across. He will use eye contact with the quarterback to signal him to deliver the ball.

Assignments

Split end: In route at 12 yards; minimum to normal split; versus man, break away; versus zone, sit out in seam or hole; make eye contact with quarterback for the ball

Tight end: Slow block; if no rush, release to flat

Flanker: Post route; normal split

Fullback: Close route, bellying back to delay entering undercoverage; hook up at 4 yards

Halfback: Hum motion; motion 5 yards outside split end, hook up at line of scrimmage

Quarterback: Presnap look; five-step drop; if WS vacates middle to go with motion, hit post; otherwise, work X to HB to FB

Versus Various Defenses

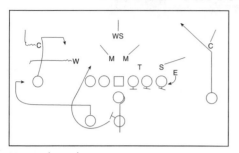

Versus three-deep

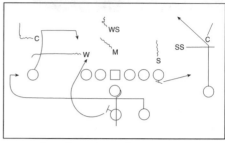

Versus four-short, three-deep (invert)

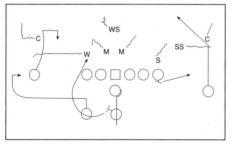

Versus invert three-deep

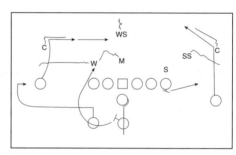

Versus man

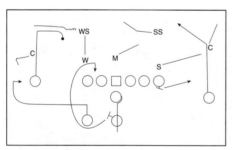

Versus roll strong

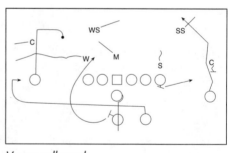

Versus roll weak

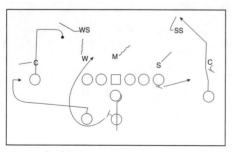

Versus double zone

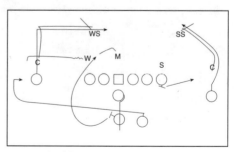

Versus double man

Spot Pass

This play is one that the San Francisco 49ers used against the Pittsburgh Steelers in 1996. It's a ball-control pass featuring a group of closely aligned receivers releasing to specific areas. Their release gives a natural pick versus man coverage. Versus zone, three receivers release to spots

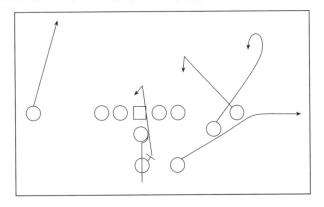

in the undercoverage for the quick pass. Because of their triangular positioning, the quarterback can find the open receiver without hesitation.

Assignments

Split end: Split route; normal split

Tight end: Take regular 3-foot split, lining up in tight slot position; release just off outside receiver coming inside; get upfield to depth of 6 yards over outside receiver's original alignment; hook up to inside; be ready for quick pass

Flanker: Line up a yard outside tight end on the line of scrimmage; release inside (you are first receiver), getting depth of 4 to 6 yards and hook up over onside tackle's area (find hole between defender over tight end and next defender inside); be ready for quick pass; in side dog, expect pass *now*

Halfback: Immediately release out on shoot route, except make your break at the line of scrimmage; expect the ball on the break

Quarterback: Presnap look; 5 quick steps on drop; work Z1 to Y2 to HB3

Fullback: Check; release on checkdown

Versus Various Defenses

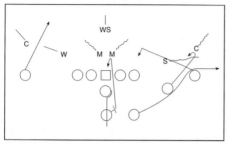

Versus three-deep

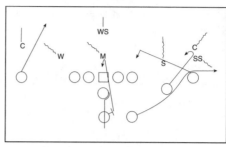

Versus four-short, three-deep (invert)

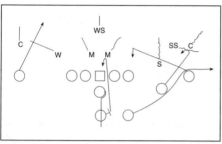

Versus invert three-deep

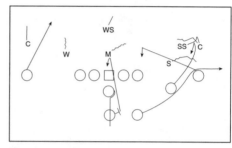

Versus man

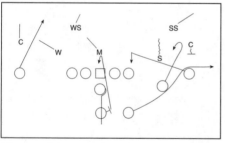

Versus roll strong

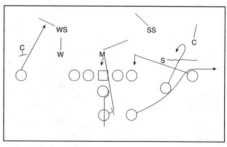

Versus roll weak

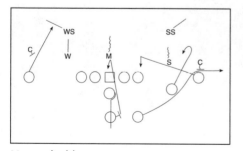

Versus double zone

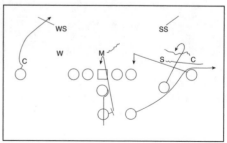

Versus double man

Play-Action Passing

Play-action passing is an essential part of the West Coast offense. It can slow down the rush, control the movement of linebackers to allow one-on-one coverage with the wide receivers, get defenders moving the wrong way, and allow the offense to immediately release a back out on route. Play-action passing can change the launch point for the quarterback, moving him out of the pocket.

This kind of passing can be more effective in neutralizing a defense than any one block. Whereas a great block can eliminate two defenders, a great play-action fake can affect many defenders. A back who carries out a great fake can freeze a defense or fool them entirely. It is this fake by the back that is the *most important key!*

The back must hit his landmark so that the quarterback can mesh well with him. He must form a big pocket with his arms and hands so that the quarterback can put the ball in and then withdraw it. As the ball is withdrawn, the back folds over his top arm and keeps his shoulders low as he carries out his fake. Keeping his shoulders low prevents the defense from easily seeing that he does not have the ball.

The quarterback must get his eyes on the pocket of the faking back. He sets the ball after the snap by bringing the ball to his midsection and fakes the ball at waist level. As he meshes with the back, the ball is extended into the back's pocket with both hands and then withdrawn with both hands, letting the far hand secure it while the near hand continues the fake. The quarterback then sets up quickly at the proper depth and delivers the pass.

Play-action passes need to come off the favorite running plays of the offense. They are effective on first down or in any running situation. They can be most effective in the goal-line offense when the defense is very quick to react to run action.

Line splits are important, since the offense does not want any defensive penetration while the quarterback has his back to the defense. Tighter splits need to prevail over larger ones.

Fullback Slant

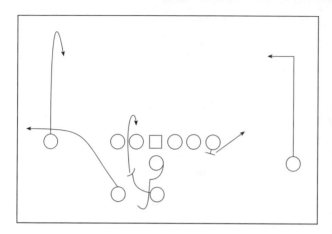

The fullback slant pass attacks the weakside, releasing the halfback out on route. It allows the offense to get the ball quickly to the half-back, who is in position to run with it after the catch. A good fake to the fullback freezes the linebackers and enables the halfback or split end to get open.

Assignments

Split end: Maximum split; run turn-in route at 14 yards; find open seam

Tight end: Regular split; slow block; if no rush, release out on route

Flanker: Maximum split; run in route at 14 yards

Fullback: Fake fullback slant action; check with linebacker for rush; block rush; if no rush, release through line and run stop route

Halfback: Release out on fan route; threaten block on linebacker, get upfield, and break to sideline; look for ball on break

Quarterback: Presnap look; pivot and mesh with fullback, making good fake; remember that your fake can fool most of the defense, so make it as excellent as possible; set up quickly and work H1 to X2 to Z3.

The line takes a minimum split to stop any defensive pene-tration.

Power Pass

The power pass gets line-backers and safeties flowing to the ball. This enables receivers to find open areas for the reception. A good fake by the quarterback and halfback allows the receivers to get open.

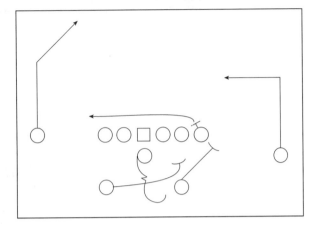

Assignments

Split end: Normal split; run post route

Tight end: Regular split; brush block and run sneak route; get past linebackers

Flanker: Maximum split; run in route at 14 yards; be aggressive coming inside

Fullback: Drive on end man (linebacker); hit into him and sustain block

Halfback: Fake power; set up for block protection on inside backer strongside; sprint across and set up

Quarterback: Presnap look; make good fake and set up quickly; work X1 to Y2 to Z3

Waggle Pass

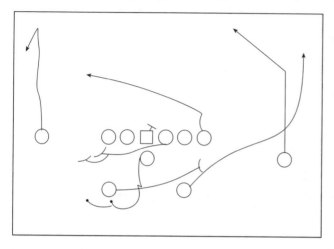

The waggle pass has the flow of the backs going strongside with the quarterback going weakside. This play allows the quarterback to move outside toward the weakside of the formation and change his launch point. The offside guard pulls to the inside of the waggle with the hole called to designate the launch point of the pass.

Assignments

Split end: Normal split; run comeback route at 15 to 18 yards; get defender running upfield thinking takeoff; run fade versus roll-up cornerback

Tight end: Regular split; run over route; be ready to hand in open area weakside

Flanker: Normal split; run post route

Fullback: Drive on end man (linebacker); release on shoot and upfield

Halfback: Fake strongside power play; good fake and block end man

Pulling guard: Pull for called launch point; G7, block any defender outside your tackle; 8 and 9, launch point is wider; stay on feet

Quarterback: Presnap look; open to halfback; make good fake and roll behind pulling guard; if 6 or 7 call, pull up and work Z1 on post to F2 on shoot and upfield; if 8 or 9 call, work X1 to Y2

Bootleg Pass

In the bootleg pass the flow of the backs goes weakside and the quarterback goes strongside. The offside guard pulls to the side of the bootleg with the hole called, designating the launch point of the pass.

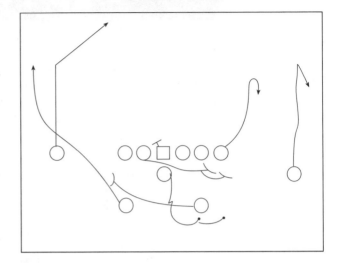

Assignments

Split end: Normal split; post route

Tight end: Stop turn-out at 10 to 12 yards; find open area

Flanker: Normal split; run comeback route at 15 to 18 yards; get defender running upfield thinking takeoff; run fade versus roll-up cornerback

Fullback: Fake weakside slant play; good fake and block end man

Halfback: Drive on end man, release on shoot and upfield

Quarterback: Presnap look; open to fullback; fake and roll behind pulling guard; 6 and 7 pull up and work X1 to H2; 8 or 9 call, work Z1 to Y2

Screen Pass and Draw Play

The number one enemy of the passing game is the hard pass rush. The screen pass and draw play are two important plays that the offense can use to counteract the defense's eagerness to get to the quarterback. These two plays need to be practiced as much as any key or major play in the offense. Many coaches view the screen and draw simply as situation plays. This is a mistake. A well-run screen pass draw is very difficult for the defense to react to and will make sizeable gains or score. For these plays to succeed, the offense must sell the dropback pass, and players must make and sustain their blocks. The advantage for the offense lies in the fact that the defense is reacting for pass, playing into the hands of the offense, and upon reading screen pass or draw must react **back** to run.

Figures 7.10 and 7.11 illustrate the assignments for the halfback screen and fullback draw.

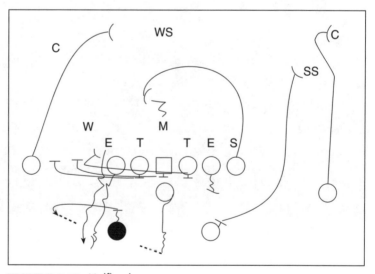

FIGURE 7.10 *Halfback screen*

Assignments (Screen)

Split end: Take a maximum split; drive off, block weakside

Outside tackle: Dropback pass protection up to 7 yards, then battle defender

Onside guard: Set up quick; block three counts, release outside, getting eyes on any defender attacking from the outside

Center: Set up, block three counts; release along line to a point 3 yards outside of the onside tackle; block any defender attacking screen wall

Offside guard: Set up; block three counts; release and set up in screen wall; expect an inside defender to attack the screen wall

Tight end: Release inside and peel back on far inside linebacker

Flanker: Drive off and peel back on cornerback

Quarterback: Take five-step drop and look downfield to force coverage to drop; set up, give ground, and put ball on screenback; if he is covered, throw ball away

Fullback: Set up; check for dog; circle outside and block undercoverage

Screenback: Step up and show block technique; if dog, block him for the three counts and release behind screen wall; if no dog, key your guard and release out when he goes out; release inside your tackle; yell "Go!" when ball leaves quarterback's hand; when breaking downfield, be wary of cutting back into pursuit; stay with wall

Assignments (Draw)

Split end: Drive off and block weakside

Onside tackle: Set up and invite man to outside; if defender goes inside or stays on line, drive block him

Onside guard: Covered, set up short, block man where he wants to go; allow no inside penetration; uncovered, set up short, release on backer, sustain your block

Center: Versus noseguard, set up and make square-up hit

Offside guard: Set up short, take defender when he wants to go; versus backer, set up, release on backer and sustain the block

Offside tackle: Set up pass block defender

Tight end: Drive block end man with inside number hit

Quarterback: Normal dropback, look downfield to sell pass, on third step look to back's pocket, hand off, continue drop

Halfback: Set up, check for dog; release out on Will backer

Fullback: Slide laterally inside outside foot, then inside foot; receive ball and break to daylight; versus even, look key guard's block; versus odd, look key center's block

Flanker: Dive off and block cornerback

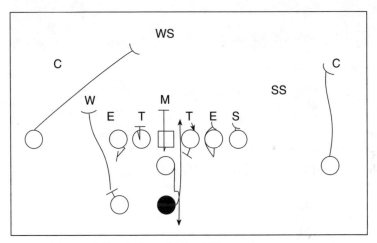

FIGURE 7.11 *Fullback draw (right side)*

Versus a split 4-4 look the center will block the onside middle backer while the halfback blocks the offside middle backer (see figure 7.12).

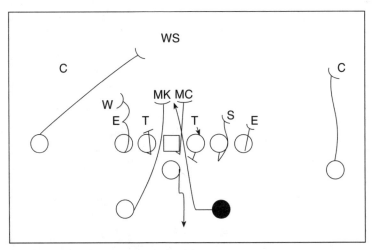

FIGURE 7.12 *Draw versus split 4-4*

Playbook Summary Chart

Play	Page No.	Coverage	Primary Emphasis or Attack
Quick Out	116	Zone or Man	Corners; Flat
Slant	118	Zone or Man	Flat
Tight End Option	120	Man	Undercoverage
Halfback Option	122	Man	Undercoverage
Fullback Option	124	Man	Undercoverage
Turn-In	126	Zone or Man	Undercoverage
Turn-In Route From Slot	128	Zone	Undercoverage
Speed Out	130	Zone or Man	Corners; Flat
Corner	132	Zone or Man	Corners
Tight End Bench	134	Zone or Man	Flat
Tight End Delay	136	Zone or Man	Undercoverage
Vertical Stretch	138	Zone or Man	Undercoverage
Strongside Flood	141	Zone or Man	Undercoverage
Shallow Route Plays	143	Zone or Man	Undercoverage

Play	Page No.	Coverage	Primary Emphasis or Attack
Post Vertical Stretch	146	Zone or Man	Undercoverage
Weakside Flood	148	Zone or Man	Weakside
Smash Option	151	Zone or Man	Cornerback; Undercoverage
Dash Pass	153	Zone or Man	Cornerback; Undercoverage
70 Series With Halfback Motion	155	Zone or Man	Weakside
Spot Pass	157	Zone or Man	Undercoverage
Fullback Slant	160	Zone or Man	Flat (weakside)
Power Pass	161	Zone or Man	Undercoverage
Waggle Pass	162	Zone or Man	Cornerback; Undercoverage
Bootleg Pass	163	Zone or Man	Cornerback; Undercoverage

About the Authors

Authors Frank Henderson and Mel Olson coached football at Brigham Young University (BYU), where over the years head coach LaVell Edwards has revolutionized the passing game. Henderson was a graduate assistant coach for BYU and has more than 20 years of coaching experience. Olson was BYU's offensive line coach for 20 years.

After serving on the BYU staff, **Frank Henderson** went on to success in the high school ranks in Utah. He served as defensive coordinator at Layton High School, helping that school win the league and state championships. At Provo High School (Utah) during his 11 years as head coach, Henderson directed his pass-oriented teams to 89 wins against only 39 losses, six league titles, and a Utah state championship. Henderson was selected Utah High School Coach of the Year by the state coaches association.

A student of the game, Henderson has spent hours studying BYU game film and has learned the passing game from such luminaries as Bill Walsh, Mike Holmgren, Chuck Knox, and Ted Tollner.

Henderson has authored articles for *Scholastic Coach* magazine. He earned an MS degree from Brigham Young University in 1977. A secondary school teacher, Henderson is a recipient of a Golden Apple Teaching Award from the Provo High School PTA.

He and his wife Nina live in Orem, Utah. His favorite leisure time activities include reading and researching, enjoying sports, weight training and exercising.

Mel Olson was offensive line coach for Brigham Young University for 20 years, during which BYU won 13 Western Athletic Conference titles and a national championship in 1984. During these years, BYU regularly led the nation in passing offense. In 1983 BYU's Cougars led all NCAA Division I teams with 584 yards offense per game. During Olson's tenure, BYU produced such quarterbacking stars as Steve Young, Jim McMahon, Marc Wilson, Giff Nielsen, and Ty Detmer. Olson coached future NFL all-pro lineman Bart Oates and Outland Trophy winner (for the nation's outstanding offensive lineman) Mohammed Elewonibi.

Olson turned in a sparkling football career as a player at BYU. A three-year starter, he had the rare distinction of being named all-conference on both sides of the ball—as a linebacker and as an offensive center.

Olson is a member of the American Football Coaches Association. He also is an instructor for the American Sport Education Program (ASEP). He holds an EdD from Brigham Young.

Olson serves as vice president of sports in the Southwest District of the American Alliance for Health, Physical Education, Recreation and Dance (AAHPERD). He also is on an AAPHERD committee to promote national coaching standards, and the National Advisory Committee for the National Association for Sport and Physical Education (NASPE) to help set national coaching standards.

Olson and his wife Susan live in Orem, Utah. They have five children: Michael, Kristen, Melissa, Tresa, and Chad. His favorite leisure time activities are golf, fishing, and hiking.

More winning game plans

1995 • Paper • 216 pp
Item PAFC0869 • ISBN 0-87322-869-3
$18.95 ($28.95 Canadian)

Football Coaching Strategies is an invaluable source of football wisdom. Inside find 67 informative articles contributed by many of the greatest football coaches the game has ever known.

The book features 349 detailed diagrams and covers every crucial aspect of the game:

- 28 articles on offense;
- 19 articles on defense;
- 7 articles on special teams; and
- 13 articles on philosophy, motivation, and management.

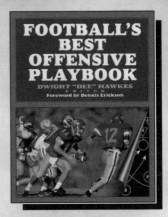

1995 • Paper • 144 pp
Item PHAW0574 • ISBN 0-87322-574-0
$15.95 ($22.95 Canadian)

Every offensive playbook gives Xs and Os that look good on paper. *Football's Best Offensive Playbook* goes the extra yard, providing precisely illustrated plays that are proven point-producers in games.

Each of the 100 running, passing, and special plays comes with a clear, accurate diagram and coaching pointers that highlight key player positions and responsibilities. Many coaches list alternate formations, and most of the plays can be adapted to any offensive system.

To request more information or to place your order, U.S. customers call TOLL FREE 1-800-747-4457. Customers outside the U.S. place your order using the appropriate telephone number/address shown in the front of this book.

Prices are subject to change.

Human Kinetics
The Premier Publisher for Sports & Fitness
http://www.humankinetics.com/

2335

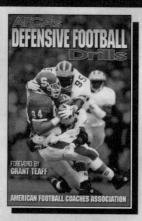
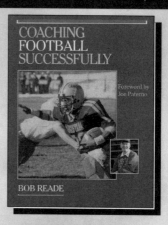